Life During the Crusades
The Way People Live

Titles in The Way People Live series include:

Cowboys in the Old West
Life Among the Great Plains Indians
Life Among the Indian Fighters
Life During the Crusades
Life During the French Revolution
Life During the Great Depression
Life During the Renaissance
Life During the Russian Revolution
Life During the Spanish Inquisition
Life in a Japanese American Internment Camp
Life in Ancient Greece
Life in Ancient Rome
Life in an Eskimo Village
Life in the Elizabethan Theater
Life in the North During the Civil War
Life in the South During the Civil War
Life in the Warsaw Ghetto
Life in War-Torn Bosnia
Life on a Medieval Pilgrimage
Life on an Israeli Kibbutz

THE WAY PEOPLE LIVE

Life During the Crusades

by Earle Rice Jr.

Lucent Books, P.O. Box 289011, San Diego, CA 92198-9011

Library of Congress Cataloging-in-Publication Data

Rice, Earle.
    Life during the crusades / by Earle Rice Jr.
        p.   cm. — (The way people live)
    Includes bibliographical references and index.
    ISBN 1-56006-379-3 (alk. paper)
    1. Crusades—Influence.   2. Europe—Social life and customs.
    3. Civilization, Medieval.   I. Title.   II. Series.
    D160.R53   1998
    909.07—dc21   97-27994
                                                                              CIP
                                                                              AC

Printed in the U.S.A.

Contents

Discovering the Humanity in Us All

The Way People Live series focuses on pockets of human culture. Some of these are current cultures, like the Eskimos of the Arctic; others no longer exist, such as the Jewish ghetto in Warsaw during World War II. What many of these cultural pockets share, however, is the fact that they have been viewed before, but not completely understood.

To really understand any culture, it is necessary to strip the mind of the common notions we hold about groups of people. These stereotypes are the archenemies of learning. It does not even matter whether the stereotypes are positive or negative; they are confining and tight. Removing them is a challenge that's not easily met, as anyone who has ever tried it will admit. Ideas that do not fit into the templates we create are unwelcome visitors—ones we would prefer remain quietly in a corner or forgotten room.

The cowboy of the Old West is a good example of such confining roles. The cowboy was courageous, yet soft-spoken. His time (it is always a he, in our template) was spent alternatively saving a rancher's daughter from certain death on a runaway stagecoach, or shooting it out with rustlers. At times, of course, he was likely to get a little crazy in town after a trail drive, but for the most part, he was the epitome of inner strength. It is disconcerting to find out that the cowboy is human, even a bit childish. Can it really be true that cowboys would line up to help the cook on the trail drive grind coffee, just hoping he would give them a little stick of pep-

permint candy that came with the coffee shipment? The idea of tough cowboys vying with one another to help "Coosie" (as they called their cooks) for a bit of candy seems silly and out of place.

So is the vision of Eskimos playing video games and watching MTV, living in prefab housing in the Arctic. It just does not fit with what "Eskimo" means. We are far more comfortable with snow igloos and whale blubber, harpoons and kayaks.

Although the cultures dealt with in Lucent's The Way People Live series are often historically and socially well known, the emphasis is on the personal aspects of life. Groups of people, while unquestionably affected by their politics and their governmental structures, are more than those institutions. How do people in a particular time and place educate their children? What do they eat? And how do they build their houses? What kinds of work do they do? What kinds of games do they enjoy? The answers to these questions bring these cultures to life. People's lives are revealed in the particulars and only by knowing the particulars can we understand these cultures' will to survive and their moments of weakness and greatness.

This is not to say that understanding politics does not help to understand a culture. There is no question that the Warsaw ghetto, for example, was a culture that was brought about by the politics and social ideas of Adolf Hitler and the Third Reich. But the Jews who were crowded together in the ghetto cannot be understood by the Reich's politics. Their life was a day-to-day battle for existence, and the creativity and methods they used to prolong their lives is a vital story of human perseverance that would be denied by focusing only on the institutions of Hitler's Germany. Knowing that children as young as five or six outwitted Nazi guards on a daily basis, that Jewish policemen helped the Germans control the ghetto, that children attended secret schools in the ghetto and even earned diplomas—these are the things that reveal the fabric of life, that can inspire, intrigue, and amaze.

Books in The Way People Live series allow both the casual reader and the student to see humans as victims, heroes, and onlookers. And although humans act in ways that can fill us with feelings of sorrow and revulsion, it is important to remember that "hero," "predator," and "victim" are dangerous terms. Heaping undue pity or praise on people reduces them to objects, and strips them of their humanity.

Seeing the Jews of Warsaw only as victims is to deny their humanity. Seeing them only as they appear in surviving photos, staring at the camera with infinite sadness, is limiting, both to them and to those who want to understand them. To an object of pity, the only appropriate response becomes "Those poor creatures!" and that reduces both the quality of their struggle and the depth of their despair. No one is served by such two-dimensional views of people and their cultures.

With this in mind, The Way People Live series strives to flesh out the traditional, two-dimensional views of people in various cultures and historical circumstances. Using a wide variety of primary quotations—the words not only of the politicians and government leaders, but of the real people whose lives are being examined—each book in the series attempts to show an honest and complete picture of a culture removed from our own by time or space.

By examining cultures in this way, the reader will notice not only the glaring differences from his or her own culture, but also will be struck by the similarities. For indeed, people share common needs—warmth, good company, stability, and affirmation from others. Ultimately, seeing how people really live, or have lived can only enrich our understanding of ourselves.

For God and Glory

The Roman Empire fell in A.D. 476. For almost six hundred years thereafter, Rome and Constantinople—the seats of the Western and Eastern branches of Christianity, respectively—vied with each other for dominance. Each wanted to become the single leader of a unified Christian Church. Ultimately, their power struggles and irreconcilable theological differences resulted in a permanent schism between the two factions. Thus, in 1054, the Christian Church split into the Roman Catholic (or Latin) Church, under the pope in Rome, and the Greek Orthodox Church, led by the bishop in Constantinople (now Istanbul).

The Greek or Eastern empire became known as the Byzantine Empire, after Byzantium, a Greek colony once located in the region. Both the Western and Eastern empires shared a common classical Greek influence. In contrast to the Christian West, however, many of the Eastern empire's dominant cultural influences also derived directly from its Middle Eastern heritage.

Meanwhile, the rise and spread of Islam —the Muslim religion founded by Muhammad the Prophet in A.D. 610—had progressed at a phenomenal rate. By the mid–eleventh century, the Islamic Empire rimmed the southern and eastern shores of the Mediterranean Sea and stretched from Spain to India, unified by a commonality of faith and the Arabic language.

Although Palestine fell under Muslim rule in 638, many Christians and Jews continued to inhabit the Holy Land. With few exceptions, the Muslims had governed mildly, allowing freedom of worship and access to religious

Pilgrims on their way to a religious shrine. During several centuries of Muslim rule Christian pilgrims were allowed free access to the Holy Land.

Battle of Manzikert

On August 19, 1071, the forces of Byzantine emperor Romanus IV Diogenes and Seljuk Turk sultan Alp Arslan clashed at Manzikert (Malazgirt, Turkey) in a pivotal battle that became a precursor to the Crusades. In A Dictionary of Military History, *historians R. Mantran and John Childs synopsize the battle this way:*

"Romanus advanced his army of heavy cavalry in a single line, supported by a strong rearguard. The Turks withdrew steadily but their mounted archers constantly harried the Byzantine flanks. Although human casualties were probably few, many Byzantine cavalrymen lost their mounts. The advance continued until dusk when Romanus ordered his army to return to camp. However, the flanks did not understand the signals and the army began to collapse in confusion. This was turned into chaos when Romanus, now separated from his rearguard and wings, continued to advance with his center as the rearguard began to retreat towards the camp. The Turks attacked and defeated the separated and disorganized sections of the Byzantine army in detail. Virtually all of Romanus's army was killed or captured, with the exception of the rearguard."

shrines to members of the other faiths. Moreover, both the Latin and Greek Churches encouraged Christians to make pilgrimages to the Holy Land as a way of absolving their sins. Such pilgrimages, unhindered by the Muslims, grew steadily in number during the first millennium after Christ, reaching close to twelve thousand people by 1064–1065.

But early in the eleventh century, the Fatimid caliph al-Hakim—the Muslim spiritual and civil leader of Egypt—began persecuting Christian pilgrims. Shortly afterward, increasingly aggressive Turks started interfering with Christian pilgrimages to Palestine. As the century drew to a close, a clash between Islam and Christianity appeared both inevitable and imminent.

Alexius Pleads for Help

During the tenth century, the wandering Turks from the plains of Central Asia adopted the religion of Islam. A century or so later, the Seljuk Turks, an aggressive group among the Turkish hordes, advanced to the West and began threatening the balance of power between the Byzantines and the Muslims in the Near East.

In 1071, during a major battle at Manzikert (now Malazgirt, Turkey), the Seljuk Turks, led by Sultan Alp Arslan, crushed the forces of Byzantine emperor Romanus IV Diogenes. Jerusalem fell to the Turks that same year. The Turks subsequently overran nearly all the Byzantine provinces in Asia Minor, stopping only a hundred miles short of Constantinople itself.

Alexius I Comnenus, who had served in the army of Romanus IV, ascended to the Byzantine throne in 1081. Of Alexius, historian Robert Payne, a superbly skilled storyteller, writes: "He was an able commander in the field and uncompromising in his determination to regain the lost provinces of his empire."[1] During his thirty-eight-year reign, Alexius managed to recapture some of the lost provinces. But after two decades of fighting, his empire still faced a struggle for survival.

Alexius appeals to the leader of Venice for help against the Turks. Alexius wanted to recover territory that had been seized by the Turks and needed the cooperation of the princes in the West.

Alexius became convinced that he would never be able to recover all of his lost territory in Asia without military aid from the West. Because of the rift that existed between the Latin and Greek empires, Alexius realized that the West might be more readily persuaded to engage in a holy war for Christ than to bear arms in support of Alexius. Accordingly, he appealed to Pope Urban II and to the Western princes for military aid, imploring them to join his war against the Muslim Turks under the banner of Christendom. In 1093, in a letter to Robert, count of Flanders—a letter reviewed later by Urban II, the papal head in Rome—Alexius first recounted atrocities committed by the Turks and then wrote:

Therefore in the name of God and because of the true piety of the generality of Greek Christians, we implore you to bring to this city all the faithful soldiers of Christ . . . to bring me aid and to bring aid to Greek Christians. . . . Before Constantinople falls into their power, you should do everything you can to be worthy of receiving heaven's benediction, an ineffable and glorious reward for your aid. It would be better that Constantinople falls into your hands than into the hands of the pagans. This city possesses the most holy relics of the Savior [including] . . . part of the True Cross on which he was crucified.

Alexius's letter went on to describe Constantinople's "wealth of treasure" that "no words can describe," ending with:

Come, then, with all your people and give battle with all your strength, so that all this treasure shall not fall into the hands of the Turks and Pechenegs [half-brothers to the Turks in Asia Minor]. . . . Therefore act while there is still time lest the kingdom of the Christians shall vanish from your sight and, what is more important, the Holy Sepulcher [Christ's tomb in Jerusalem] shall vanish. And in your coming you will find your reward in heaven, and if you do not come, God will condemn you.

If all this glory is not sufficient for you, remember that you will find all those treasures and also the most beautiful women of the Orient. The incomparable beauty of Greek women would seem to be a sufficient reason to attract the armies of the Franks [Europeans] to the plains of Thrace [a region in the Balkan peninsula extending to the Danube].[2]

From the enticement offered in his last paragraph, it appears that Alexius was leaving nothing to chance in his efforts to enlist the West's participation in a holy war waged in his own behalf.

Urban II Calls for a Crusade

Ironically, perhaps, the concept of holy war, or *jihad*, originated in the Islamic world and in its earliest application represented a form of Muslim expansionism. "The military clash between religions has often proved a potent inspiration for warriors," asserts French military historian André Corvisier. "Islam and Christianity have both fought each other in holy wars although the degree and nature of their motivation has differed."[3]

In Arabic the word *Islam* means "surrender" or "submission," hence the submission of the true believer to the will of Allah, the one God. The word *jihad* often forms a part of the phrase *Jihad fi Sabil Allah*, meaning "effort directed along the path of God." Muhammad the Prophet exhorted the *jihad* as one of the five obligations of the true believer. Taking part in a *jihad* ensures entrance into paradise to the faithful Muslim who falls in battle. In Corvisier's view, "The *Jihad* is the driving force and justification for the battle of Islam against unbelief."[4]

Eventually, Christians borrowed a page from the Prophet's canon, as Corvisier explains:

Christianity has also fought to convert or exterminate non-believers. The clearest examples were the wars fought by Charlemagne against the Saxons, conflicts which were later carried on by the Knights of the Teutonic Order against Prussia and the Baltic lands. After achieving conversion, these wars degenerated into conquest. The Crusades to the Holy Land were different in character. Their deeper origins are found in the ecclesiastical prescriptions of the ninth century which sanctified battle against the infidel [unbeliever with respect to a particular

Muhammad, prophet of Islam, expounds his creed to the faithful. Adherents of Islam believed it was their duty to battle nonbelievers.

religion] in order to protect Christians who were suffering oppression.[5]

Prior to the Church's ninth-century sanctions, Christianity generally opposed warfare as being counter to the major themes of its religious doctrine. Although St. Augustine of Hippo (354–430) had argued for "the *legitimacy* of war under certain specified conditions," Christians only reluctantly accepted his conditional justification of war. According to Edward Peters, professor of medieval history at the University of Pennsylvania, they "had never regarded warfare as in any way virtuous and often expressed concern for the possible salvation of those who killed enemies in battle."[6]

Over time, however, as Marcus Bull, a prominent historian of the crusading movement, points out:

The standard position [of the Church on violence], which became associated with Augustine and was refined in later centuries, was that the moral rectitude of an act could not be judged simply by examining the physical event in isolation: violence was validated to a greater or lesser degree by the state of mind of those responsible, the ends sought, and the competence of the individual or body which authorized the act.

Thus allowed considerable ideological flexibility, the Church was able to take an active interest in warfare on a number of fronts, including those areas where Latin Christendom came into direct contact with the Muslim world.[7]

Almost three years after Alexius I Comnenus's appeal to the Latin West for help, Pope Urban II, empowered by such "ideological flexibility," called on his Frankish countrymen to mount a crusade against the Muslim infidels in the Holy Land.

"God Wills It!"

On November 27, 1095, following a church council meeting in Clermont, in Auvergne (a former province in south-central France), a vast assemblage of churchmen, knights, and laypeople gathered in a spacious field just outside the city walls. From an elevated platform in their midst, Urban II, speaking in French, "called on Frankish knights to vow to march to the East with the twin aims of freeing Christians from the yoke of Islamic rule and liberating the tomb of Christ, the Holy Sepulcher in Jerusalem, from Muslim control."[8] Robert Payne explains:

> It was not by any means a sudden call based upon an emotional sympathy for the Christians who had suffered in Asia Minor and the Holy Land. It was more, and it was less. Urban II was asserting the pope's

leadership in the West, he was attempting to dominate the quarreling princes of Europe by declaring a holy war in the East and the Truce of God in the West, and he was trying to give direction to a divided Europe at a time when quarrels were becoming dangerous not only to the papacy but to the very survival of Christendom. . . . By the Truce of God he meant to outlaw fighting of any kind from Sunday to Wednesday, and to put an absolute ban on fighting involving priests, monks, women, laborers, and merchants on any day of the week. At Clermont the pope was able to impose a further ban on fighting on certain religious holidays [and seasons such as Advent and Lent]. There was some irony in

This fourteenth-century French illustration depicts Pope Urban II's arrival in France (left) and the Council of Clermont (right). Urban urged the Frankish knights to march against the Turks and to take control of Jerusalem.

The Deeds of Brave Men

Whether crusaders sought personal gain, absolution for their sins, or merely the satisfaction of serving God, their reward was often an early death in a faraway land. But their brave deeds lived on to inspire others. In the prologue of his Chronicle of the First Crusade, *the eleventh-century cleric Fulcher of Chartres scribed:*

"It is especially pleasing to the living, and it is even beneficial to the dead, when the deeds of brave men (particularly of those serving as soldiers of God) are either read from writings or soberly recounted from memory among the faithful. For, after hearing of the deeds of faithful predecessors who rejected the beauties and pleasures of the world and clung to God, and in accordance with the precept of the Gospel, left their parents and wives and possessions, however great, to follow Him, those here on earth are inspired to serve Him more eagerly in that same spirit. It is beneficial to the dead, especially to those dead in the Lord, when the living, upon hearing of their good and devoted work, bless their faithful souls, and out of love bestow alms with prayers on their behalf whether they were known to them, or not."

the fact that the pope who called so strenuously for peace in France was also calling for a holy war in the Holy Land.[9]

Five major versions of the pope's speech have been recorded and handed down through time. Will Durant, the late, great American chronicler of the ages, called Urban's plea "the most influential speech in medieval history." One version of the pope's eloquent call to arms concludes with a plea to Europe's quarreling factions to end their differences and unite in a holy cause:

Let hatred, therefore, depart from among you; let your quarrels end. Enter upon the road to the Holy Sepulcher; wrest that land from a wicked race, and subject it to yourselves. Jerusalem is a land fruitful above all others, a paradise of delights. That royal city, situated at the center of the earth, implores you to come to her aid. Undertake this journey eagerly for the remission of your sins, and be assured of the reward of imperishable glory in the Kingdom of Heaven.

"Through the crowd," writes Durant, "an excited exclamation rose: *Dieu li volt!*—'God wills it!' Urban took it up, and called upon them to make it their battle cry."[10]

In 1096–1097, upward of fifty thousand Christian soldiers answered Urban's call. And for God and glory the followers of Christianity clashed with the disciples of Islam in the first of eight crusades that spanned three centuries.

Life in the Christian West

In considering the Crusades, many historians, scholars, and writers emphasize the romantic aspects of the Holy Wars. History's scribes often focus on mounted knights in gleaming armor, sallying forth with sword and lance to fight the good fight for God and glory. Writers of romantic novels tend to portray all enemies of Christendom as hated infidels who sought to stamp out not only Christianity, but all that was good in a world lit only by fire. More often than not, of course, the truth generally lies somewhere in between the extremes.

Except for occasional oblique references to life beyond the fields of valor, however, more than a few chroniclers of the crusading past have left to the reader's imagination the details of daily living of both Christians and Muslims during that fascinating period. Yet, to clearly understand the concept of crusading and the motivations of those on both sides who took part in the Crusades, it is essential to examine the nature and quality of day-to-day life in the Christian West and the Muslim East.

"The Great Task of Feudalism"

The soldiers of Christ went off to fight their holy wars with the Saracens (a broad term for Muslims or Arabs) for a variety of reasons, both spiritual and material. According to medieval historian Sherrilyn Kenyon:

Men yielded to the church's call out of religious fervor (indulgences were granted for participants), desire for gold and land, because debts were postponed until a crusader returned, and for honor and glory, and other human reasons. . . . Many men seized upon [the] notion of a divinely sanctioned war and used it to their own purposes.

And as in all wars—both then and now, holy or otherwise—money, or the lack of it, is the key enabling factor. In the case of the crusading knight, Kenyon writes,

the average cost of a knight going on a crusade was four to five times his yearly income. Money was needed for care of his horses, pack animals, servants and armor. Money could be gained in a number of ways: taxation, sale of land and goods, and loans. Dr. Elizabeth Hallam has stated that it would be virtually impossible for a landless knight to raise the money needed unless he was in the employ of a wealthier lord.[11]

The knight, although a significant figure in the feudal system of the Middle Ages, represented only a slim segment of the medieval population in Europe. Feudalism was a social system of rights and obligations that established classes based on land-ownership patterns. About nine-tenths of the people living under the feudal system were peasants, farmers, or village laborers. Of the feudal organization, Will Durant writes:

> In those lands and times society consisted of freemen, serfs, and slaves. Freemen included nobles, clerics, professional soldiers, practitioners of the professions, most merchants and artisans, and peasants who owned their land with little or no obligation to any feudal lord, or leased it from a lord for a money rent. Such peasant proprietors constituted some four per cent of the farming population of England in the eleventh century; they were more numerous in western Germany, northern Italy, and southern France; they probably constituted a quarter of the total population in Western Europe.[12]

Feudalism blossomed in an age of disorder where the central government had failed in its fundamental purpose of protecting its citizenry. Building on the basic precept of land tenure, feudalism gave rise to a new, highly structured way of life, ruled by the nobility, protected by knights and foot soldiers, and serviced by laypeople. "The great task of feudalism was to restore political and economic order to Europe after a century of disruptive invasions and calamities," Durant surmises. "It succeeded; and when it decayed, modern civilization rose upon its ruins and its legacy."[13]

Crusaders leave for Palestine in an attempt to take the Holy Land from the Saracens. Many knights participated in the Crusades in hopes of financial gain.

The Birth of Feudalism

The Western Roman Empire fell in the year 476. That year—more often rounded off to 500—marks the beginning of the Middle Ages, which are generally categorized as the millennium between 500 and 1500. A scattering of barbarian kingdoms arose out of the breakup of Rome's ancient empire, the kings of which warred continually with one another.

Charlemagne (742–814), king of the Franks, the Germanic tribe that conquered Gaul (France), tried to build a new Christian empire in Rome's image. By 800 he had become undisputed ruler of western Europe. He succeeded in restoring much of the unity of the old Roman Empire and paving the way for the development of modern Europe. But upon Charlemagne's death in 814, in the absence of a strong successor, his empire fell into decay amidst civil wars and revolts.

Unable to defend themselves in the face of constant dangers from barbarian invaders and others, people naturally began turning to their strongest neighbors—landholding nobles—for protection. But nobles wanted a fee for providing protection. And because money was in short supply, they willingly agreed to accept land in payment for their protective services. Thus feudalism was born.

Charlemagne, king of the Franks, tried to model a Christian kingdom after Rome.

The Center of Feudal Life

Before and even during the rise of towns in medieval Europe, the manor constituted the basic economic and administrative unit in England, northern France, and elsewhere. The manor, which varied in size, was presided over by a lord and constituted the center of feudal life. As described by James Harpur—a scholarly writer and editor specializing in history, religion, and mythology—a manor typically consisted of a village or villages whose nucleus was formed by the lord's castle or residence, a church, and the houses and hovels of peasants. There were also generally two or three large arable fields, common and waste land, and woodland, all of which belonged to the manor.

Fields were split up into small strips, some of which were granted to the peasants for cultivation, while the others made up what was called the lord's demesne

The Feudal Pyramid

Feudalism in its broadest sense was the holding and working of land by giving one's service to the owner. Technically, it was a system of political organization used during most of the Middle Ages, based on the relation of lord to vassal with all land held in fee.

A king receives his vassal. The king was at the top of the feudal pyramid.

It was characterized by homage, the service of tenants under arms and in court, wardship, and forfeiture.

A vassal vowed homage (respect and services) and fealty (loyalty) to a feudal lord in return for protection and the use of land owned by the lord. Under feudal law, a vassal forfeited his rights to tenancy and the lord's protection for failing to uphold his sworn obligations. Also, when a lord acted as guardian of a minor, he retained the right to hold and use the ward's land, as well as all accrued profits, until the minor came of age at twenty-one. Sometimes a vassal would sublease part of his tenured land (land held in return for services, and so on). The sublessee would then become a vassal to the vassal.

This intricate interrelationship among landholders formed a pyramidal social structure, with the king or state at the pinnacle and descending to lord and thence to vassal and possibly even to several sublevels of vassalage, hence the term "feudal pyramid."

[land held for the lord's own use as opposed to tenured land]. . . .

The manor was generally self-supporting and required few goods from the outside —usually only salt, to preserve meat; iron for implements; and luxury goods for the lord. And the community was served by the necessary specialist craftsmen, for instance blacksmiths, potters, millers, and cobblers.

In return for the lord's protection, the peasants were bound to farm his demesne for a specific number of days per week— usually two or three—as well as extra days at sowing and harvest time. Although the peasants were poor, they still had to pay the lord for certain services and permissions. For example, they paid rent for their dwelling places—usually in the form of a pig or a chicken or two; for having their grain ground at the lord's mill; or for marrying a daughter to someone from another manor. In addition to all this, they had to give a tenth, or a tithe, of their produce per year to the parish priest for the support and upkeep of the local church.[14]

The lord of the manor generally employed a bailiff to assist him in managing his estate. The bailiff oversaw day-to-day activities and sometimes kept the manorial accounts. With the help of senior villagers, he also judged manor dwellers accused of petty crimes.

Castle Life

A lord's castle or fortified manor house provided some measure of protection against aggressive interlopers, but only the strongest castles built during the Middle Ages were capable of withstanding a strong assault or a sustained siege. As historian Peter Draper points out:

> The majority of fortified structures . . . ranging from the grandest castles to fortified manor-houses, were primarily demonstrative. . . .

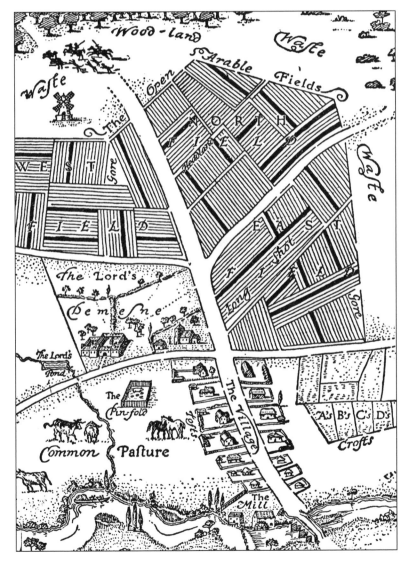

The layout of a typical medieval manor, including the surrounding land where crops and livestock were raised.

The building of one or more towers on a manor-house may have afforded some means of defense against a small-scale attack or riot, but the number and size of the towers were more significant as a reflection of feudal status, of the owner's relationship with his superior lord. . . .

External appearance was important in all these houses, but the sense of grandeur was also expressed in the interior, mainly in the Great Hall, which served a variety of public functions. The grandest of these halls were aisled, some having stone or marbled piers [vertical structural supports]. . . . Many of them also had impressively elaborate timber roofs, splendid tiled floors and from the late thirteenth century magnificent traceried [ornamented] windows.[15]

Earlier medieval castles were not quite so sumptuous, however, as even a cursory examination of life in an eleventh-century castle reveals. For example, Philip Warner, a military historian and lifelong student of castles, writes:

Home-life in the castle was based on the hall. . . . The floor would be covered with rushes, dogs, scraps of food, bones, and dirt. Food was prepared and cooked out of doors; there was too much risk in having ovens in wooden buildings. [Early castles were built of earth and wood.]

. . . European castles were, for most of the year, cold, wet, and murky. Damp and dark could not easily be countered in the absence of heating, but cold could be alleviated by clothing. . . . Castle-dwellers wore their bed covers as garments. The wealthier people were able to have theirs lined with furs, of which ermine was a fa-

vorite, and remains a distinction of aristocracy today. Poorer people would be lucky if they had wool at all, let alone fur to line it with. The wealthier went to bed naked and the luckier ones had curtains around their four-posters. Poorer people wore their clothes day and night, and had little to put on their beds.[16]

A castle household, in addition to the lord and lady of the manor and their children, comprised a staff that varied in size with the wealth of the lord. Some household staffs numbered more than sixty servants. The quantity of foodstuffs required to sustain such a large staff constituted a substantial expense, even for the wealthiest lord.

A lord's family (pictured) made up only a small portion of the members of his entire household.

A table set for a baron's household. The wealthy in medieval society ate three meals a day and were served a variety of foods.

Daily Bread and Other Sustenance

"An everyday dinner," write Joseph and Frances Gies, well-known chroniclers of medieval life and times, "served between 10:00 A.M. and noon, comprised two or three courses, each of several separate dishes, all repeating the same kinds of food except the last course, which consisted of fruits, nuts, cheese, wafers, and spiced wine." Yet such substantial fare paled in comparison to the typical feast served on holidays and festive occasions. The Gies offer the following example:

When Henry III's daughter married the king of Scotland on Christmas Day 1252 at York, Matthew Paris [a Benedictine monk noted for his chronicles of the thirteenth century] reported that "more than sixty pasture cattle formed the first and principal course at table . . . the gift of the archbishop. The guests feasted by turns with one king at a time, at another time with the other, who vied with one another in preparing costly meals." As for the entertainment, the number and apparel of the guests, the variety of foods: "If I were

more fully to describe [them] . . . the relation would appear hyperbolical [greatly exaggerated] in the ears of those not present, and would give rise to ironical remarks." Such feasts included boars' heads, venison, peacocks, swans, suckling pigs, cranes, plovers, and larks.[17]

Aside from special occasions, three meals—breakfast, dinner, and supper—were served daily at the castle. "Supper at the castle was a light meal served at sunset and usually consisted of one main dish, several small side dishes and cheese," writes Sherrilyn Kenyon, who further notes:

After supper, castle occupants might be entertained by a traveling minstrel, acrobat, contortionist, jongleur or storyteller who performed for their food and were usually given coins as well. If no professional entertainers were present, games might be played, or the lady of the hall or a knight might provide entertainment with a song, instrument or story.[18]

Peasants fared less well in the food choices available to them under their frequently impoverished conditions. "An average

Peasants milk livestock and churn butter. The manor was completely self-sufficient, with peasants to work the land and process all of the crops.

meal consisted of porridge, turnips, dark bread (only the nobility had white bread), and beer or ale," Kenyon recounts, continuing:

> A salad might be added that would consist of parsley, borage, mint, rosemary, thyme, purslayne, garlic or fennel. During hog slaughtering season, peasants would eat pork and bacon, but usually fish was the primary source of meat.
>
> Villagers would eat bread—either rye, barley or wheat—that was occasionally mixed with peas or beans. They also enjoyed oatmeal cakes, porridge, fish, cheese curds, watery ale, mead [an alcoholic drink of fermented honey and water], cider and metheglin [a kind of mead]. . . .

All medieval dishes relied heavily on spices for a number of reasons, the largest being that spices covered the taste of spoiling meat. Garlic was used so heavily by the French that the crusaders of-

fended the people of Constantinople with their breath![19]

Just as the usual diet of villagers and peasants, be they freemen or serfs (that is, people who owned or leased land as opposed to those bound to the service of a lord), compared unfavorably with that of castle householders, their average dwelling also fell considerably short of living conditions in the lord's castle or manor house.

Village Life

A peasant village might house anywhere from ten to sixty families. "The village rural household raised its own vegetables [90 percent of the feudal economy was agricultural] and some of its meat, spun its wool or linen, made most of its clothing," writes Will Durant.

> The village blacksmith hammered out iron tools, the tanner made leather goods, the carpenter built cottages and furni-

ture, the wheelwright made carts; fullers [cloth craftsmen who cleansed and thickened newly woven fabrics], dyers, masons, saddlers, cobblers, soapmakers . . . lived in the village or came there transiently to ply their crafts on demand; and a public butcher or baker competed with the peasant and the housewife in preparing meat and bread.[20]

In most cases the peasant built his own house. Each family lived in a hovel that provided minimal creature comforts at best. The typical peasant dwelling was

a dark, dank hut made of wood or wicker daubed with mud and thatched with straw or rushes. Layers of straw or reeds covered the floor, fouled by the pigs, chickens, and other animals housed with the family. The one bed was a pile of dried leaves or straw. All slept in their rough garb, with skins of animals for cover. A cooking fire of peat or wood burned drearily in a clearing on the dirt floor. The smoke seeped out through a hole in the roof or the open half of a two-piece door. The only furniture was a plank table on trestles, a few stools, perhaps a chest, and probably a loom for the women to make their own cloth. Every hut had a vegetable patch.[21]

The mistress of the peasant household made all the family's clothes, mostly of wool or linen. Typical attire included a tunic, gathered about the waist with a leather cord, a cap, pants called breeches, and long stockings, usually pulled up over the pant legs and gartered. Peasants generally wore leather shoes in winter but went barefoot or wore wooden clogs in summer. Neither nobles nor peasants wore undergarments or nightclothes until late in the Middle Ages.

Peasants harvest grain for the lord of the manor. A peasant's life consisted of hard labor and long hours.

"Very little separated the dress of the nobility from that of the peasantry," avers Sherrilyn Kenyon. "The styles of clothing and the types of fabric they wore were very much alike." Kenyon attributes the similarity "mostly to limited trade caused by poor travel conditions." Nobles managed to set themselves apart from common folk, however, relying on jewels, which were more readily available in many areas, "especially in the North [of England], where mining was prevalent."[22]

Hardships abounded in the daily lives of medieval peasants, but, as many historians maintain, perhaps no more so than in the lives of today's peasants. Interestingly, because of the many holy days (holidays) in the Middle Ages, peasants actually worked only about 260 days a year. According to Will Durant, on Sundays and holy days

> the peasant sang and danced, and forgot in hearty rustic laughter the dour burden of sermon and farm. Ale was cheap, speech was free and profane, and loose tales of womankind mingled with awesome legends of the saints. Rough games of football, hockey, wrestling, and weight throwing, pitted man against man, village against village. Cockfighting and bullbaiting flourished; and hilarity reached its height when, within a closed circle, two blindfolded men, armed with cudgels, tried to kill a goose or a pig. Sometimes, of an evening, peasants visited one another, played indoor games, and drank; usually, however, they stayed at home, for no streets were lit; and at home, since candles were dear, they went to bed soon after dark. In the long nights of the winter the family welcomed the cattle into the cottage, thankful for their heat.[23]

Clearly, life at the lowest level of the feudal pyramid was hard, sufficiently so as to encourage more than a few enterprising individuals to seek relief from its constricts. In much the same way as many of today's youth seek to better their lots on athletic playing fields or courts, many of their medieval predecessors sought to similarly improve their fortunes on more lethal fields of tournaments and conflict. Knighthood, for those who could meet its challenge, offered both enhanced respectability and the chance to become a member of the landed gentry.

CHAPTER 2

Soldiers of the Cross

Knighthood flowered long ago under the feudal system, before the advent of guns and gunpowder finally rendered the sword and lance ineffective and the knight obsolete. Yet legends of the knight continue to charm the fancy of new generations drawn to the chivalric notions of an earlier day. Some such notions ring of truth and reality; some do not. The writings of acclaimed medieval historian Frances Carney Gies help to separate truth from fiction in the Western world's enduring fascination with knights:

> Of all the many types of soldier that have appeared on the military stage in the course of time, from the Greek hoplite, the Roman legionary, and the Ottoman janissary to members of specialized branches of modern armed forces, none has had a longer career than the knight of the European Middle Ages, and none has had an equal impact on history, social and cultural as well as political. . . .
>
> The institution of knighthood summons up in the mind of every literate person the image of an armor-plated warrior on horseback, with the title "Sir," whose house was a castle, and who divided his time between the pageantry of the tournament and the lonely adventures of knight-errantry. The image has the defect of being static, and it represents a concept that belongs more to legend and literature than to real life. Yet the real his-

torical figure of the knight is not totally at odds with the popular image. He did indeed wear plate armor, but plate superseded mail only late in his long career. The "Sir"—"Messire" in French—also came late and in England still exists as a title of honor or of minor nobility. A knight sometimes lived in a castle, but the castle was rarely his own. He participated in tournaments, but the tournament's character as pageant developed only in its decadence. He was certainly prone to adventure in his often short life, but nearly always in company and in search of income rather than romance.[24]

In short, even knights needed to earn a living. And though a knight's life was often short, the lack of preparation and training could hardly be faulted in the event of his early demise.

Training for the Knighthood

Training for the knighthood was mentally and physically tough and demanding. "The youth who aimed at knighthood submitted to a long and arduous discipline,"[25] declares Will Durant. His education began at an age that finds present-day youths still engaged in less serious pastimes involving space marauders, turtlelike masters of martial arts, rollerized street hockey, and so on, and it continued for about eight years.

A fourteenth-century fresco shows combat between two knights at a tournament. A knight's training was rigorous and lasted about fourteen years.

At age seven, an aspirant to a life behind a lance was uprooted from his home and sent to live in a castle, often that of his father's lord, where he served as a page to the lord and his lady. The page waited on his hosts at the dinner table and accompanied them to various affairs, available to render services as needed to his lord and lady. A castle chaplain schooled him in religion, and resident squires introduced him to arms training. Under the tutelage of his mistress and her ladies, he learned to honor and protect all women. He learned to sing and to play the flute; to hunt and to hawk. Most important, he learned to ride a horse. When a page successfully completed his early knightly apprenticeship at the age of fourteen, he was elevated to squire.

"Squire" is the shortened form of "esquire," derived—via *esquier* (Old French)—from the Latin *scutarius*, or shield-bearer. Thus, in the context of knighthood, a squire is defined as "one who carried the shield of a knight and ranked immediately below him."[26] As a squire, the young man learned to handle the sword and the lance, to bear the bulk and weight of armor, and to serve the general needs of the knight assigned to him.

Much of the squire's training was focused on physical conditioning and on hardening him to the pain and stresses that he might encounter in future conflicts. Commenting on such training, Roger of Hoveden, a twelfth-century English chronicler who accompanied Richard the Lionheart on his crusade to the Holy Land, wrote: "A youth must have seen his blood flow and felt his teeth crack under the blow of his adversary and have been thrown on the ground twenty times—thus will he be able to face real war with the hope of victory."[27]

Since ceremony marked the service at the dinner table,

> part of a squire's training [as well as a page's] was learning how to serve his lord

The Squire

In his prologue to The Canterbury Tales, *twelfth-century author Geoffrey Chaucer deftly portrays a youthful squire this way:*

In stature he was of average length,
Wondrously active, aye, and great of
    strength. . . .
Short was his gown, with sleeves both
    long and wide.
Well could he sit on a horse, and fairly
    ride. . . .
And he was clad in coat and hood of
    green,
A sheaf of peacock arrows bright and
    keen
Under his belt he wore carefully
(Well could he keep his tackle yeo-
    manly:

His arrows had no draggled feathers
    low),
And in his hand he bore a mighty bow.
A cropped head had he and a sun-
    browned face. . . .
Upon his arm he wore a bracer [pro-
    tector] gay,
And at one side a sword and buckler,
    yea,
And at the other side a dagger bright,
Well sheathed and sharp as a spear
    point in the light;
On breast a Christopher [medal] of sil-
    ver sheen.
He bore a horn in baldric [shoulder
    belt] all of green;
A forester he truly was, I guess.

A knight, his horse, and page ready themselves for a tournament. A page, or knight-in-training, began his education at age seven.

at meals: the order in which dishes should be presented, where they should be placed, how many fingers to use in holding the joint for the lord to carve, how to cut the trenchers [an edible bread platter used instead of a plate] and place them on the table.[28]

A squire—usually, but not always, a knight in training—was responsible for polishing and maintaining in good repair the arms, armor, and equipment of his knight and the armor and accoutrements of his knight's horses. But a squire's duties went far beyond the scope of his training within the friendly confines of the castle.

It was the faithful squire who accompanied his knight into every fray, assisting him in donning his armor and mounting his horse. It was he who stood by his knight in the clutch of mortal circumstance, always ready to bear

The Knighting Ceremony

A squire and knight in typical attire of the First Crusade. After serving many years as a page and squire, a young man could become eligible for knighthood.

a hand or wield a sword if his knight became overmatched, or lend his steed should the knight lose his own. And it was the squire who bore responsibility for carting off his master's body should wounds disable or death claim the knight on the battlefield. Such were but a few of the many lessons learned and the innumerable duties and responsibilities shouldered by the youthful knight-aspirant.

At about age twenty-one, assuming a creditable performance as page and squire, the successful candidate became eligible to accept the vows of knighthood. More than a few knights-to-be, perhaps, underwent the elaborate knighting ceremony mindful of the musings of Roger of Hoveden: "The reward for hours of toil waits where the temples of victory stand."[29]

Ostentation and symbolism marked the knighting ceremony. "Rituals associated with 'knighting' were based on royal coronations," write British military historians Nicholas Hooper and Matthew Bennett. "The giving of arms, particularly tying on the sword belt (a symbol of knighthood), was an ancient bond between lord and follower."[30] Will Durant, the articulate dean of American historians, calls the ceremony "a ritual of sacramental awe" and characterized it this way:

> The candidate began with a bath as a symbol of spiritual, perhaps as a guarantee of physical, purification; hence he could be called a "knight of the bath," as distinguished from those "knights of the sword" who had received their accolade on some battlefield as an immediate reward for bravery. He was clothed in a white tunic, red robe, and black coat, representing respectively the hoped-for purity of his morals, the blood he might shed for honor or God, and the death he must be prepared to meet unflinchingly.

For a day prior to his knighting, the candidate fasted and spent the night in church. He prayed, confessed his sins to a priest, took communion, heard a sermon on the several obligations of a knight—moral, religious, social, and military—and solemnly vowed to discharge them. Thus prepared, the knight-aspirant

> then advanced to the altar with a sword hanging from his neck; the priest removed the sword, blessed it, and replaced it upon his neck. The candidate turned to the seated lord from whom he sought knighthood, and was met with a stern

question: "For what purpose do you desire to enter the order? If to be rich, to take your ease, and be held in honor without doing honor to knighthood, you are unworthy of it, and would be to the order of knighthood what the simoniacal clerk is to the prelacy [that is, as one who buys or sells high religious office is to church government]." The candidate was prepared with a reassuring reply.

Attendant knights or ladies then adorned the candidate with a knightly array consisting of hauberk (tunic of chain mail), cuirass (breastplate), armlets, gauntlets (armored gloves), sword, and spurs. Gold spurs symbolized the ranking of a knight, while silver spurs signified the status of a squire; therefore to "win his spurs" (of gold) meant to achieve knighthood. The ceremony concluded with the so-called dubbing rite.

The lord, rising, gave him the accolade [that is, on the neck]—three blows with the flat of the sword upon the neck or shoulder, and sometimes a slap on the cheek, as symbols of the last affronts that he might accept without redress; and "dubbed" him with the formula, "In the name of God, St. Michael, and St. George I make thee knight." The new knight received a lance, a helmet, and a horse; he adjusted his helmet, leaped upon his horse, brandished his lance, flourished his sword, rode out from the church, distributed gifts to his attendants, and gave a feast for his friends.[31]

The newly dubbed knight had now earned the right to participate in tournaments. The tournament served both as a spectacular showcase of knightly prowess and daring deeds and as a mock-combat training

A knight takes a solemn oath during a dubbing ceremony. Such ceremonies were patterned after a king's coronation and were extremely elaborate.

ground for knights to hone their fighting skills and horsemanship and further condition themselves for the rigors of real warfare.

Tournaments

Often after a knighting ceremony, the host lord held a tournament, a colorful, lavish, and sometimes brutal form of entertainment. Knights from miles around were invited to participate and often came in such numbers that the lord's castle overflowed with guests and tents were pitched alongside the tourney field, or lists, to accommodate latecomers.

Tournaments are said to have been invented by Geoffrey of Preuilly, a Frenchman who died in 1066. "With their pageantry and color, banquets and dances, tournaments took on the atmosphere of a carnival, with all the associated trappings," writes historian James Harpur, an expert on medieval affairs. "And they drew the full gamut of medieval characters, from armorers, harness makers, and horse dealers to moneylenders, fortunetellers, and prostitutes."[32] Tourney competitions initially resembled actual warfare, except that losing opponents were captured and ransomed rather than killed. They usually featured single engagements between two knights—tilting or jousting—either on horseback or on foot. Occasionally, however, large group contests held sway, closely simulating the dust and din of real martial engagements.

A knight is officially dubbed. After the ceremony, a knight participated in a tournament to display his skills as a horseman and fighter.

A jousting tournament turns into murder as one knight goes too far, stabbing his opponent beneath his armor. Such slayings were fairly uncommon, as jousting tournaments were mainly for demonstration purposes only.

Although touted as sporting competitions, the mock battles sometimes turned ugly and more than a few knights were slain. According to military historian Michael Prestwich, "Tournaments were celebrations of an international chivalric culture, and while in glorifying knighthood they undoubtedly assisted and encouraged enthusiasm for war, there was no necessity to turn them into nationalistic festivals."[33] Nevertheless, once in a while, displays (or threatened displays) of spirited nationalism among contestants necessitated the cancellation of tournaments in the interest of public safety. Moreover, incidents involving knights and nobles ganging up on individual foes and using the melee as a cover for murder were not unknown.

During the thirteenth century—encouraged by the use of lighter armor, blunted weapons, and formalized rules—a newer, gentler kind of tournament called a *plaisance* evolved, that is, a pleasant tourney fought only for show. The church, which had long condemned tournaments for misdirecting knights from the service of God, smiled on this development.

By the fifteenth century, only the pageantry and spectacle of the tournament remained. Not long afterward, with the decline of feudalism and the advent of artillery—which drastically changed the makeup of armies and the strategies and tactics of warfare—the era of knighthood ended. But not before the knight of chivalric creed emblazoned a romantic and virtually untarnished image for all time in history's book of the brave and the bold.

Chivalry and *Chevauchées*

Alfred Lord Tennyson used only nine words to summarize the code of chivalry: "Live pure, speak true, right wrong, follow the king."[34] His economical use of words reflects the poetic grace that brought him acclaim but falls far short of fully defining the complexities of the chivalric creed. His terse summation lacks even a hint of chivalry's darker side. "Contrary to the popular view of undisciplined knights, the military values they celebrated were prudence, cunning, and caution, as well as bravery," assert military historians Nicholas Hooper and Matthew Bennett. "Thus, 'chivalric' commanders were masters of ambushes, sudden attacks, night marches, and deceptions." Continuing, Hooper and Bennett go on to explore the limits of chivalrous conduct:

> Chivalry was not unique in appreciating courage, loyalty, generosity, and military skill. The special quality of chivalry was that a vanquished fellow knight was spared: instead of death or slavery, which he might have expected in the seventh century, for example, he would be ransomed. However, this code only governed relationships between knights, so relatively few were killed when knight fought knight. Non-knights or "barbarians," for example common infantry or the Welsh, Irish, or pagan Slavs, were not covered by it. . . . Outside this [knightly] group, chivalry did little to limit the brutality of war. The plundering raid (*chevauchée*), the normal practice of chivalric warfare, was aimed at the civilian population in order to put pressure on their rulers, much as indiscriminate "area bombing" was in the Second World War.[35]

Despite the widespread human suffering wrought by the pillaging and torching conventions of the *chevauchée*—literally, a French term meaning "to be on horseback"—no dishonor was associated with its practice. Quite to the contrary; at least in the view of Count Philip of Flanders, who, according to Jordan Fantosme in his *Chronicle*, advised military commanders in 1173:

> *Destroy your foes and lay waste their country,*
> *By fire and burning let all be set alight,*
> *That nothing be left for them, either in wood or meadow,*
> *Of which in the morning they could have a meal.*
> *Then with his united force let him besiege their castles.*
> *Thus should war be begun: such is my advice.*
> *First lay waste the land.*[36]

More than two hundred years later, Britain's king Henry V echoed Philip's advice. "War without fire," he said, "is like sausages without mustard."[37] And for the next six centuries, belligerents continued—and continue yet—to use fire as a condiment for ravaging the populations and scorching the lands of their enemies.

Foot Soldiers All

It might also be said that war without foot soldiers is like no war at all. Historically, the romantic image of the knight has disproportionately claimed whatever glamour and glory can be culled from the blood and gore of medieval wars. Actually, however, most battles and wars have ultimately been won by the relatively lowly foot soldier. Tales accentuating the importance of the omnipotent knight in medieval warfare are often steeped in mythology rather than in reality. Bernard S. Bachrach, a professor of history specializing in the period just prior to the Crusades, declares:

There was a romantic time not long ago when it was generally believed that medieval warfare consisted of undisciplined fief-holding [land or estate holding in return for services rendered] warriors, irrationally driven by their chivalric ethic, fighting an individualistic style of combat dominated by battles between single knights who engage in mounted shock combat. This view is false. . . .

[M]ost important in creating a highly misleading picture of the medieval military in all its aspects, the romantic epics known as the *chansons de geste* portrayed the mounted knight as dominating medieval

Warhorses

A knight rides his warhorse, a horse especially adept in battle. The warhorse often wore sweat padding and protective armor, covered by elaborate trappings bearing the owner's coat of arms.

Horses represented the most essential elements of a knight's equipment. In Armies and Warfare in the Middle Ages, *military historian Michael Prestwich comments on several breeds of horses:*

"The warhorse was the most expensive possession of a knight or man-at-arms. A destrier, the most specialized of warhorses, was not an ordinary animal. It was a highly trained, expertly bred beast, capable of carrying an impressive load of man and armor in the terrifying conditions of battle. . . . Coursers were another highly prized type of horse. More ordinary animals were described [as] rounceys, or simply as *equi*, or horses. All of these were suitable for use in war; in general, warhorses were clearly quite distinct from palfreys, or riding horses, and from the various types of farm horses. . . .

Men needed more than just one horse; important men needed a considerable number. Horses might become sick or lame, and remounts were needed. Warhorses were not suitable for riding long distances; a knight would possess at least two other horses in addition to his charger."

warfare and more particularly the battle-fields of Europe—much as the "Westerns" of the American cinema show the cowboy conquering the frontier with his six-gun. Neither image is true. Medieval literary entertainment and medieval games popularized and magnified the importance of the man on horseback, and their posterity has for too long accepted fiction and play as reality.

Nor were knights, according to Bachrach, opposed to perpetuating their own mythic image:

The willingness of those men in the middle ages, who saw themselves as the military elite, to propagate the myth that they were the essential feature of a medieval army through song and story, and even through the patronage of "historians" and artists, is noteworthy. Nevertheless, the "feudal host" of "knights" serving their lords for forty days in return for fiefs [land for services] was, in general, of relatively little importance in medieval military organization. . . . Furthermore, the training of militias for local defense, together with the support of levies of foot soldiers and substantial numbers of archers and crossbowmen for offensive military operations throughout medieval Europe, clearly indicate the importance accorded to such units by those who formulated military policy or grand strategy.

"Finally," concludes Bachrach, in relegating the knight to his actual rather than mythical role in the medieval military hierarchy, "the training of mounted troops to fight on foot

A knight and common soldiers of the First Crusade. The bulk of the crusaders' armies was made up of foot soldiers.

and the dominance of siege warfare provide more than a subtle hint regarding the multifaceted nature of medieval warfare in which sieges dominated and the knight of romantic literature was but one figure in a very complex equation."[38]

So, as the soldiers of the Cross forayed toward the Muslim East to recapture the Holy Land for the Christian West, it should come as no surprise that their ranks swelled with archers, crossbowmen, spearmen, foragers, and fire-raisers—foot soldiers all—outnumbering horsemen by ratios of five or six to one. The role of foot soldiers was no less vital in medieval times than it is today. No war has ever been won without them.

Life in the Muslim East

As the eleventh century drew to a close, the Islamic and Byzantine civilizations flourished in the East, while the Christian West floundered in economic decline and struggled to recover from a series of barbarian invasions. Observed the late Will Durant:

> For five centuries, from 700 to 1200, Islam led the world in power, order, and extent of government, in refinement of manners, in standards of living, in humane legislation and religious toleration, in literature, scholarship, science, medicine, and philosophy. In Islam art and culture were more widely shared than in medieval Christendom. . . .
>
> The Moslems [Muslims] seem to have been better gentlemen than their Christian peers; they kept their word more frequently, showed more mercy to the defeated, and were seldom guilty of brutality. . . . Christian law continued to use ordeal by battle, water, or fire while Moslem law was developing an advanced jurisprudence and an enlightened judiciary. The Mohammedan religion [Islam], less original than the Hebrew, less embracing in eclecticism [selection of the best of various doctrines] than the Christian, kept its creed and ritual simpler and purer, less dramatic and colorful than the Christian, and made less concession to the natural polytheism [belief in many gods] of mankind. . . .
>
> The influence of Christendom was almost limited to religion and war.[39]

Contrary, perhaps, to popular present-day imaginings, the world of Islam at the onset of the Crusades represented a civilization much more advanced than its Western counterpart.

The elaborate interior of a mosque reveals the Muslims' artistic abilities. In culture, art, and law, Muslims exceeded the accomplishments of their Christian counterparts.

The Islamic World

Unlike the predominantly rural population groupings that clustered about the widely scattered estates of feudal lords in the West, much of the Muslim populace was concentrated in cities unrivaled in their day in both size and splendor. For example, according to French historian Georges Tate, the Muslim world

> boasted splendid cities like Baghdad, Damascus, and Antioch, especially in Syria and Mesopotamia [the area between the Tigris and Euphrates Rivers], where the tradition of urban life went back thousands of years. The cities were all laid out along the same design; a mosque and markets in the center of town and, in the principal cities, a ruler's palace; they were surrounded by ramparts and crowned by a citadel [a fortress that commands a city]. As seats of international or long-distance commerce and centers of regional exchanges, they figured among the largest cities in the world, some with hundreds of thousands of inhabitants. Western cities, by contrast, tended to be administrative and religious settlements, rather than trading centers.[40]

Arabs constituted an overwhelming majority of the Muslim populace. About 20 percent of their numbers wandered the deserts and trade routes of the Middle East and North Africa. Members of wandering tribes are called nomads, or Bedouins. They lived (and still live) in tents and traveled by camel, existing primarily by tending flocks of camels, sheep, and goats. Most Arabs, although descended from nomadic tribes, lived on farms or resided in the bustling cities of minarets, mosques, and bazaars (towers, temples, and markets), engaged in business and commerce.

According to Islam, Muhammad recorded divine revelations in the Koran, from which the laws of Muslim civilization are derived.

Islamic Laws

Whether city dwellers, farmers, or desert wanderers, the religion of Islam represented the most powerful force in the lives of all Muslims. Islamic laws derive from the divine revelations accorded to Muhammad in the seventh century and as such are virtually immutable. The laws of Islam governed not only their relations with Allah (God) but also their relations with one another.

Of all the Islamic laws, those regulating human relations—marriage, divorce, parental care, and the like—were the ones most universally observed. "Until the nineteenth century A.D.," notes John Alden Williams, a doctor of philosophy who lectures on Islamic history, "the general tendency of the *'ulama'* [scholars] was to expand the practical application of the Law—already in theory eternal and universal—so as to give religious value to every act and aspect of life."[41] Personal relations begin at home with the family and therefore so do the laws governing them.

The Arab Family

As in most cultures, the family is the basic unit of Arab society. The Arab family, as well as everything else in Arab life, is male dominated. Male dominance is emphatically established in the Koran, the Muslim holy book equivalent to the Christian Bible, and remains in place to this day. The Koran states:

> Men have authority over women because Allah [God] has made the one superior to the others, and because they spend their wealth to maintain them. Good women are obedient. They guard their unseen parts because Allah has guarded them. As for those from whom you fear disobedience, admonish them and send them to beds apart and beat them. Then if they obey you, take no further action against them. Allah is high, supreme. (4:34)

Accordingly, Arabs consider women to be the property of their fathers or husbands. Islamic laws governing marriage are many and complex including how they were contracted and terminated. From the teachings of the Hanifa school, the chief law school of the Ottoman and Mogul Empires, we learn that between Muslims "marriage is contracted—that is to say, is effected and legally confirmed—by means of declaration and consent," witnessed by two men or by "one man and two women

Men in typical medieval Muslim garb. Islamic society was governed by men.

who are sane, adult, and Muslim." Ending a Muslim marriage was even less complicated:

> The most laudable divorce is where the husband repudiates his wife by a single formula with her term of ritual purity (not during the menstrual period) and leaves her (untouched) to the observance of the *'idda* (period of waiting to ascertain she is not with child). . . . Express divorce is where a husband delivers the sentence in direct and unequivocal terms, as "I have divorced you," or "you are divorced." (To be final, the divorce must be pronounced three times.) This effects a reversible divorce such as leaves it in his power to take her back before the expiration of the *'idda*.[42]

Muslim women had little power to govern their lives; their role in society was to bear and rear children.

Most Muslim marriages, generally arranged for children by their parents, were monogamous—one husband and one wife—but the Koran allows the man up to four wives (4:2). Furthermore, as Will Durant observes, "Facility of divorce made it possible for a Moslem to have almost any number of successive mates; Ali [son-in-law of Muhammad] had 200; Ibn al-Teiyib, a dyer of Baghdad who lived to be eighty-five, is reported to have married 900 wives."[43]

A woman, on the other hand, was allowed to have only one husband at a time and could divorce him only at great expense. As to her options in matters of marital discord, the Koran states: "If a woman fear ill-treatment or desertion on the part of her husband, it shall be no offense for them to seek a mutual agreement [divorce settlement], for agreement is best" (4:128). A husband might routinely engage in extramarital liaisons without fear of redress, but a wife risked swift execution for her own infidelity.

For Muslim children, raised in strict observance of Islamic tenets, childhood's hour passed swiftly. Girls were taught little beyond prayers, a few chapters of the Koran, and domestic skills. Except for women of the upper classes, literacy and the pursuit of higher learning were mostly limited to male achievers. "Girls were usually married by the age of twelve, and were mothers at thirteen or fourteen; some married at nine or ten; men married as early as fifteen," reports Will Durant. Early marriages, multiple and successive wives, and the legalized, widespread use of concubines combined to create rather sizable Muslim families, prompting Durant to hyperbolize that in some cases "a man's household might contain as many children as an American suburb."[44]

Muslim Dwellings and Personal Attire

A typical Muslim town was of modest size, as a rule accommodating about ten thousand people. Quarters were cramped, usually little stucco houses with adjoining walls, built within a drab external wall for protection against attack or siege. Streets were unlit and unpaved and dusty or muddy depending on seasonal whims. More often than not, the ever-present mosque provided the only sign of architectural aesthetics. Along with the population, most of the splendor of Muslim civilization was concentrated in the cities. To illustrate, Basim Musallam, a Fellow of King's College who teaches Islamic history at the University of Cambridge, asserts:

To describe Islamic society as traditionally urban has become something of a cliché. The history of the Middle East is the history of its cities, where commerce and learning, industry and art, government and faith flourished. Its hinterland has rarely known a landed gentry with rural power bases. Power bases were urban. Tribal chiefs often formed armies from men of desert or mountain, and led them to conquer the cities. But once they established their power, their interests lay in a stable and prosperous urban life.[45]

Urban residences of the rich and powerful were in some areas constructed in solid masonry and sometimes featured attached gardens of flowers, shrubs, and fruit trees. But such homes were exceptional. Basim Musallam's description of houses in Fez, Morocco, provides a more representative example of Muslim homes:

Houses vary throughout the Islamic world according to the influence of pre-Islamic cultures, climate, geography, building materials, and construction techniques. Nevertheless, their nature is profoundly influenced by two concerns widely shared by Muslims: the right of the family to keep its affairs secure from neighborhood and state, providing it did

The Cities of Islam

"Wherever Islam spread, from Andalusia to India, its cities had certain features in common," asserts K. N. Chaudhuri, the Vasco da Gama Professor of European Expansion at the European University Institute in Florence, Italy. In "The Economy in Muslim Societies," part of The Cambridge Illustrated History of the Islamic World, *Professor Chaudhuri explains:*

"Most private houses, even in Damascus, Cairo, or Baghdad, were built with sun-dried bricks, whose fragility made the cities seem constantly dilapidated to foreign travellers. Only the architecture of power—mosques, palaces, citadels, and city walls—could make a claim to permanency by using kiln-baked bricks or cut stones. However, in the Yemen [in the southern Arabian peninsula] and many parts of Iran the town houses of the wealthy were constructed in solid masonry. The skill of Muslim architects and builders showed itself in a style that was varied by different materials but

perfectly integrated with the arid environment and the climate. The austere geometric lines of the buildings, the artistic motifs created in white plaster, and the ornate painted timber ceilings inside expressed a sensibility as unmistakably Islamic as the Quranic [Koranic] inscriptions at the entrance to a mosque. While public buildings were carefully planned and executed, the rest of the city was left completely unplanned. The original circular inner city of Baghdad was an exception. Most other Islamic towns were characterized by narrow, winding streets flanked by tall structures with very little space between them. The main streets, lined with shops, were often covered in order to provide shelter from the fierce sun in summer and rains in winter. The open space around the citadel palace and the Friday mosque—used for communal recreation, religious processions, and the display of horsemanship—compensated to some extent for the dense and solid urban landscape."

not flaunt wrongdoing, and the impact of Islamic law and Muslim preferences with regard to women.

Little can be guessed of the interior of the houses of Fez from their exterior. Tall blank walls face the outside world. If they are pierced by windows at ground level, they are small, grilled, and high enough to prevent passers by from peeping in. Windows higher up may be larger but must not overlook the courtyards of neighbors. Not a hint was to be given externally of the nature of life within. Wisdom, moreover, taught men to conceal their women from the prying eyes of neighbors and their wealth from the jealous sight of the authorities.[46]

Each house contained a segregated woman's area called a *harem* (related to *haram*, meaning "sacred") from which visitors were excluded. If the man of the house kept more than one wife, he provided separate but equal apartments for each wife.

In effect, the houses looked inwards. Resources were spent in making beautiful interiors using tilework, stucco, and wood. The family lived around a courtyard, or courtyards, where trees and lush vegetation would be grown for coolness and shade, and water might flow to cisterns and fountains.[47]

Like their houses, the attire of Muslims varied from one area to another. The affluent

The woman's area, or harem, *of a large Arab household.*

A dancer and musicians entertain bystanders on a public street.

wore white silk and carried swords; the commoner was typically garbed in a turban, shapeless trousers, and pointed shoes. Urban women attracted admiring male eyes with ensembles of tight bodices, bright girdles, and loose-fitting, gaily colored skirts. They wore veils below the eyes to screen themselves from the view of strangers, for only a woman's husband could look upon her face. In smaller towns and rural areas, women often wore dark robes and covered their faces with a shawl. Men might wear a long robe called a *jallabiyah*, with roomy pants and a long shirt, draped outside and tailing to the knees.

Food, Drinks, and Entertainment

Diners at a typical Muslim table partook of an enviable variety of foodstuffs. Some menu mainstays were secured through trade with Asia. Over time, many of them were passed along to the Christian West: rice, buckwheat, sugarcane, spinach, asparagus, olives, to name a few. And fruits abounded in the Muslim diet: pomegranates, cherries, grapes, grapefruits, quinces, strawberries, figs, dates, bananas, oranges, lemons, and more.

Meat also graced the Muslim table in abundance, except as restricted by the Koran, which states: "It is lawful for you to eat the flesh of all beasts other than that which is hereby announced to you" (5:1). The holy book goes on to list a series of edicts, of which, perhaps, the most important is:

You are forbidden carrion [dead and decaying flesh], blood, and the flesh of swine; also any flesh dedicated to other than Allah. You are forbidden the flesh of strangled animals and of those beaten or gored to death; of those killed by a fall or mangled by beasts of prey (unless you make it clean by giving the death-stroke yourselves); also of animals sacrificed to idols. (5:3)

The Koran also sanctions seafood: "It is lawful for you to hunt in the sea and to eat its fish, a good food for you and for the seafarer" (5:96). Intoxicating drinks made from fermented grapes or dates are abominations to be

Life in the Muslim East

Two Arabic men play a board game in a tent. Although Islam allowed games, it strictly forbade gambling.

avoided, but "liquor produced by means of honey, wheat, barley, or millet is lawful . . . provided it not be drunk in a wanton manner."[48]

The generally abundant availability of food and drink makes it easy to see why feasting held a prominent place in a wide range of Muslim amusements. Other popular entertainments included "flirtation, poetry, music, and song; to which the lower orders added cockfights, ropedancers, jugglers, magicians, puppets."[49] Sports of all kinds—boxing, wrestling, gymnastics, weight lifting, archery, fencing, and many more—were as big in Islam during the Crusades as they are today around the world.

Since the Koran forbade gambling, cards, dice, and other games of chance were rarely played. Horse racing enjoyed a great following among the wealthy and was patronized by the caliphs.

East and West

When Muhammad died unexpectedly in A.D. 632, Abu Bakr, his father-in-law and longtime companion, was chosen as his successor and given the title of caliph. Abu Bakr's appointment began the caliphate institution, the nominal ruling power in Islam from 632 to 1924. The title of caliph meant both "successor" and "deputy." Ibn Khaldun, a fourteenth-century Muslim law professor and judge, writes:

> In later times he has (also) been called "the sultan," when there were numerous (claimants to the position) or when, in view of the distances (separating different regions) and in disregard of the conditions governing the institution, people were forced to render the oath of allegiance to anybody who seized power.[50]

Apart from differences in their respective religions and governmental systems of caliphs and kings, Muslims and Christians shared a host of similar virtues and vices. Both Islam and Christendom experienced continual corruption among governmental and judicial bodies. Although gambling and intoxication were sternly denounced by the Koran (5:90) and more mildly condemned by the Christian Church, some gambling and much drinking continued in both cultures.

In both Eastern and Western societies, women were subservient to men. But in one regard, at least, a Muslim wife held a slight advantage over some European wives: She owned whatever property she acquired in its entirety, free of any claim of her husband or his creditors.

In business and commercial dealings, Muslims of medieval times often displayed more honesty and generally upheld a higher moral standard than Christians of that era. Muslim hospitality tended to be generous and universal, manners formal and congenial, and speech prone to effusive compliments. "Like the Jews, the Moslems greeted one another with a solemn bow and salutation: 'Peace [*salaam*] be with you'; and the proper reply of every Moslem was, 'On you be peace, and the mercy and blessings of God.'"[51] On the other side of the coin, Muslim attitudes toward unbelievers were usually no less sinister as those held by Christians toward infidels.

The Gardens of Allah

Of all the differences between East and West, perhaps no tradition more distinguishes the

---

The Meaning of the Caliphate

In the introduction (Muqaddima) *to his multivolume history of the world, the* Kitab al-Ibar, *the fourteenth-century North African philosopher-historian Ibn Khaldun explains, in effect, that every ruler who governs in accordance with the Koran is essentially a successor of Muhammad the Prophet. The following extract from his* Muqaddima *is taken from* Islam, *edited by John Alden Williams:*

"Political laws consider only worldly interests. 'They know the outward life of this world' (Koran 30:7). On the other hand, the intention of the Lawgiver has concerning mankind is their welfare in the other world. Therefore, it is necessary, as required by the religious law, to cause the mass to act in accordance with the religious laws in all their affairs touching both this world and the other world. The authority to do so was possessed by the representatives of the religious law, the prophets. (Later on, it was possessed) by those who took their place, the caliphs.

This makes it clear what the caliphate means. Natural royal authority means to cause the masses to act as required by purpose and desire. Political (royal authority) means to cause the masses to act as required by intellectual (rational) insight into the means of furthering their worldly interests and avoiding anything that is harmful (in that respect). The caliphate means to cause the masses to act as required by religious insight into their interests in the other world as well as in this world. (The worldly interests) have bearing upon (the interests in the other world), since according to the Lawgiver (Muhammad), all worldly conditions are to be considered in their relation to their value for the other world. Thus (the caliphate) in reality substitutes for the Lawgiver (Muhammad), in as much as it serves, like him, to protect the religion and to exercise (political) leadership of the world. . . .

The institute is called 'the caliphate' or 'the imamate.' The person in charge is called 'the caliph' or the 'imam.' [Later, he has also been called 'the sultan.']"

Islamic world from all others than the call of the muezzin. The muezzin, a Muslim crier, calls out and chants from a minaret or balcony at the local mosque (a house of communal worship), to summon the faithful to prayer. Five times each day his cries resonate across towns and cities—at sunrise, noon, mid-afternoon, sunset, and midevening.

Islam allows personal, spontaneous prayers to be offered at other times but considers these five prayers to be "obligatory for every Muslim who has reached puberty and has the use of reason, except women who are in their [menstrual] courses or recovering from childbirth." Ubada b. al-Samit, according to twelfth-century Islamic legal specialist Ibn Qudama, reported:

> I heard the Prophet say: "There are five prayers which God has prescribed for His servants in the space of a day and a night. He who observes the prayers has the promise of God that He will cause him to enter Paradise. He who does not perform them has no promise from God: If God wills, He will punish him, and if He wills, He will pardon him."[52]

The path to Islamic paradise clearly requires the total devotion of true believers aspiring to abide eternally in "gardens watered by running streams," as promised by the Koran (4:122).

During the last years of the eleventh century, the fervent religious dedication of Islam's adherents began to take on a new, critical relevance for soldiers of the Cross. As they gathered in answer to Pope Urban's call, they might have been well advised to peruse the Koran, for there it is also written:

Far above the city, a muezzin calls the faithful to prayer.

> Believers, be ever on your guard. March in detachments or in one body. . . .

> Let those who would exchange the life of this world for the hereafter, fight for the cause of Allah; whether they die or conquer, We shall richly reward them. (4:72–73)

At Nicaea (now Iznik, Turkey), commencing on May 14, 1097, the warriors of the crescent clashed with the soldiers of Christ, confident of victory and disdainful of death, for in their hearts they carried the promise of rich rewards and eternal life in the Gardens of Allah.

Warriors of the Crescent

Since men first banded together in opposing groups for the purposes of war, combatants on both sides have entered every fray convinced that only their own cause is favored by whatever god or gods they honor.

During the First Crusade, for example, the knights of Christ rallied to cries of *"Dieu li volt!"* ("God wills it!"), heralding their belief as to whose side God was on. At the same time, the warriors of Islam, confident of the sanctity of their own cause, rushed into battle shouting "Death to the infidels!" It is, after all, written in the Koran that "the true believers fight for the cause of Allah, but the infidels fight for idols" (4:73).

Both Christians and Muslims placed their faith in one god and fought in the name of that god; both sides were unswervingly convinced of the rightness of their fight in the eyes of that god. Only their approaches to battle differed.

The difference between the occidental and oriental military systems was fundamentally a matter of degree rather than approach, which is clearly illustrated in this passage from the works of the eminent German military historian Hans Delbrück:

> When the occidental knights held a tournament in the Holy Land, it probably happened that Moslem knights appeared in the area and were finally invited to participate in the tourney. The fact that they jousted together is proof enough that the equipment, fighting style, and combat customs were very similar on both sides. The accounts of the Crusades offer quite a number of indications that, despite all the religious and racial hatred, there was a certain similarity of the concept of classes between the Christian and Moslem knights.[53]

The Meteoric Rise of Islam

However, just as there were similarities between the combat customs of Christians and Muslims, there were also marked differences. The period between A.D. 632 and 732 marked

Muslims and Christians face off in the first battle of the First Crusade. Both sides claimed their god as their exclusive sponsor.

Warriors of the Crescent **45**

a century of dynamic change in the Mediterranean Basin and the Middle East. Inspired by the charismatic leadership of Muhammad and fired by a religious zeal unequaled in military history, Arab armies extended the limits of Islam across nearly half of the civilized world.

"No other religion has ever been able to inspire so many men, so consistently and so enthusiastically, to be completely heedless of death and of personal danger in battle," declare renown military historians R. Ernest Dupuy and Trevor N. Dupuy. "Thus it was energy more than skill, religious fanaticism rather than a superior military system, and missionary zeal instead of an organized scheme of recruitment which accounted for Moslem victories."[54]

By 732, when the Arab conquests lost momentum, the Islamic world stretched from the mountains of central Asia in the East to the Atlantic coast of Morocco in the West,

and northward into Spain and southern France. But their extraordinary advances came not without consequences, as the Dupuys point out:

Once the initial headlong rush had run its course, the Moslems began to realize that even their own religious fervor could not afford the appalling loss of life resulting from heedless light-cavalry charges—almost entirely by unarmored men wielding sword and lance—against the skilled bowmen of China and Byzantium, or the solid masses of the Franks. Having by this time come into contact with every important military system in the world, the Mohammedans sensibly adopted many Byzantine military practices. . . . Their original fanaticism, nevertheless, combined with astute adoption of Byzantine tactics and strategic methods, made them

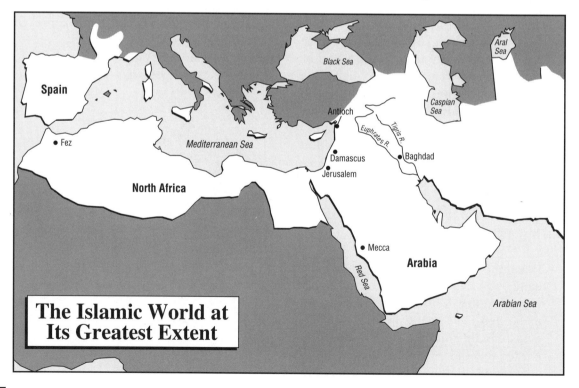

The Islamic World at Its Greatest Extent

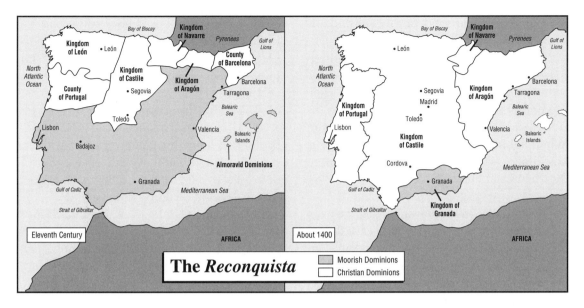

The *Reconquista*

Moorish Dominions
Christian Dominions

still the most formidable offensive force in the world at the close of this period [circa 800]. . . .

By the end of the eighth century the perimeter of Islam was generally stabilized, but endemic [native to a particular people or country] warfare persisted—and would persist for centuries—along three flaming frontiers: the mountains of Andalusia [in southern Spain], the mountains of Anatolia [the region of Turkey comprising the Asia Minor peninsula], and the mountains and deserts of central Asia.[55]

The *Reconquista*

The Arab invasion of Spain in the early eighth century wrested part but not all of the Iberian peninsula from the Visigoths. In the foothills of the Pyrenees several Christian kingdoms held fast to a precarious existence. Upon the breakup of the Umayyad Caliphate into small disparate successor states during the 1030s, the Christian states—León,

Castille, Navarre, Aragón, and the County of Barcelona—seized advantage of Arab disunity to commence the *Reconquista*—the Christian reconquest of Spain.

Although the Christians captured Valencia, the Moors maintained a presence in Spain until the armies of Ferdinand and Isabella drove them out of Granada—the last Moorish bastion in Spain—in 1492. Thus ended the *Reconquista*.

Comparing Armor, Weapons, and Tactics

"Two things gave the Christian forces in Spain superiority over their Moslem foes," aver John Matthews and Bob Stewart, specialists and frequent lecturers on Celtic and Arthurian themes, "the weight of their armor and horses, and their possession of massive siege engines." The Moors lacked siege engines, such as the powerful mangonel, which "could project massive boulders against the walls of a besieged castle"; or the trebuchet, which "could lob the lifeless carcass of a horse (or more often a human corpse) over the walls, to add to the disease already raging within."[56]

In the absence of these devastatingly fearsome machines, the Arabs "depended more on starvation tactics and in sheer weight of numbers; they scarcely ever adapted to the use of siege towers or other engines of war." When fighting on open ground, however, the advantage swung to the Arabs, as noted by Matthews and Stewart:

> The Moors' skill as horsemen and the magnificent Arab steeds they rode gave them a positive advantage over the heavily armored war-horses of the Christians, which were more like cart horses, slow and heavy against the speedy, light Arab mounts.
>
> The Moslems also wore much lighter armor and carried light swords, bows and spears. Again, these gave them the advantage when it came to the swift "attack-and-run" tactics which they frequently employed.[57]

"Arab tactics were based upon the *razzia*, the traditional Bedouin raid," observes Lawrence D. Higgins, a frequent writer on military subjects. "In fact, most campaigns [during the first century of Islam's expansion] were just a series of raids." But the *razzia* was not without defects, as Higgins explains: "After the cavalry had driven home the charge, each warrior engaged in single combat with an enemy soldier—just as if he were on an intertribal raid in Arabia. All unit cohesion disappeared."[58]

On balance, in head-on cavalry clashes, the heavily armored Christians with superior armor-piercing capabilities routinely prevailed over the more lightly armored and equipped Muslims. In the words of Matthews and Stewart, "The Christians were virtually unstoppable." Concluding their assessment of Christian and Arab fighting qualities, Matthews and Stewart write:

> Both sides made use of bows, though the Moslems were by far the more proficient in their use. In hand-to-hand fighting,

Christian knights had certain advantages over the Muslims in warfare, including the use of the mangonel, which was used to heave boulders against the walls of a castle during a siege.

The Field of Blood

Perhaps no better example of Muslim ferocity in combat can be found than a battle fought near Antioch in 1119. An invading force under Ilghazi, the emir (ruler) of Mardin, surprised and destroyed the defending army of Norman prince Roger of Antioch at Balat, west of Aleppo. In Francesco Gabrieli's Arab Historians of the Crusades, twelfth-century Muslim historian Kamal Ad-din II described the action in the battle that came to be known as the Field of Blood:

"As dawn broke [Roger's troops] saw the Muslim standards advancing to surround them completely. The qadi [religious judge] Abu l-Fadl ibn al-Khashshab was at their head, mounted on a mare and carrying a lance, and urging the Muslims on to war. One of the [Muslim] soldiers, seeing him, said scornfully: 'So we have left home and come all this way to march behind a turban [religious and legal scholars wore the turban]!' but the qadi at the head of the troops rode up and down the lines haranguing them and using all his eloquence to incite them to summon every energy and rise to the highest pitch of enthusiasm, until the men wept with emotion and admiration. Then Tughan Arslan ibn Dimlaj led the charge, and the army swept down on the enemy tents, spreading chaos and destruction. God gave victory to the Muslims. The Franks who fled their camp were slaughtered. The Turks [Muslims] fought superbly, charging the enemy from every direction like one man. Arrows flew thick as locusts, and the Franks, with missiles raining down on infantry and cavalry alike, turned and fled. The cavalry was destroyed, the infantry was cut to pieces, the followers and servants were all taken prisoner. Roger was killed, but (only) twenty Muslims were lost . . . whereas only twenty Franks escaped. A few of the leaders got away, but almost 15,000 men fell in battle, which took place on Saturday (28 June) at midday."

once again the huge and heavy broadswords of the Christians proved superior over the light, curved scimitars of their adversaries. Again, in the use of spears, the Christian knight, crouched behind his kite-shaped shield, atop his massive war horse could topple a lightly armed man completely out of the saddle—and probably spear him through in the process. . . .

In a straight fight, the Christians usually won; in skirmishes, the Moslem forces held their own and often overcame their opponents with fanatical zeal.[59]

The weapons and tactics developed over several centuries by both Christians and Muslims during the *Reconquista* hold particular relevance regarding the Crusades. As David L. Bongard points out, "The idea of the 'crusade' probably arose in Spain, as part of the warfare between Christian and Moor for control of the Iberian peninsula."[60]

And while the knights of the Christian kingdoms struggled to reclaim Spain from the Moors of Islam near the end of the eleventh century, many more thousands of Christian knights were proceeding overland and by sea toward the Holy Land, intent on giving life to the crusading idea.

Warriors of the Crescent 49

When considering the hardships and deprivations endured by the armies of Christendom along the many paths to Jerusalem, one can only marvel at how the crusaders were able to lift a lance or sword, let alone fight effectively, upon their arrival in the Holy Land. Small wonder, too, that many among their ranks—most, in fact—felt less than joyful about the prospect of a long march or voyage to the East. Jonathan Riley-Smith, professor of ecclesiastical history at the University of Cambridge, explains:

> It is now clear that most crusaders did not particularly look forward to Crusades.

They disliked leaving home: a theme in crusade poetry is sadness at the abandonment of loved ones. They dreaded the journey, especially if it was to be by sea. During the long overland marches, far from sources of regular supplies, they were often hungry and always had to forage. There was a heavy death-toll of horses and pack animals, which meant that the knights lost status and had to fight on foot, reduced to carrying their own arms and armor in sacks over their shoulders. The marches were made bearable, it seems, only by ritualization, a constant round of processions, prayers and

A thirteenth-century painting depicts a ship carrying knights across the Mediterranean to fight in the First Crusade.

even fasting, which had the effect of binding the crusaders together and helping to alleviate their feelings of homesickness and isolation. Then there were the dangers inherent in fighting in an age before tetanus injections or antibiotics, when even a small scratch could lead to a painful and lingering death.

The dependents of crusaders left at home also suffered great distress, explains Riley-Smith:

> Their families and properties were supposed to be protected by the Church and State during their absence, but neither body was particularly effective in this respect. Wives and relatives struggling to manage farms with several of the men away were always at a disadvantage. Campaigning in the East would generally involve an absence of at least two years—or two harvests—which was enough to ruin any agricultural business. No wonder contemporary [medieval] writings were filled with the anxieties of crusaders' families.[61]

It is likely that few experiences shared by the crusaders and the loved ones they left behind caused more anxiety than the moment of their parting. And perhaps no medieval scribe portrays the panoply of human emotions attendant to sad farewells better than Fulcher of Chartres.

Sadness and Joy

Fulcher of Chartres, a member of the clergy, accompanied the entourage of Stephen, count of Blois, on the First Crusade. In chapter V of his three-volume *Chronicle* of that crusade, Fulcher writes of poignant partings:

As crusaders march off to fight the Muslims, family and friends pray for their success and safe return.

> Oh, how much grief there was! How many sighs! How much sorrow! How much weeping among loved ones when the husband left his wife so dear to him, as well as his children, father and mother, brothers and grandparents, and possessions however great!
>
> But however so many tears those remaining shed for those going, these were not swayed by such tears from leaving all that they possessed; without doubt believing that they would receive an hundredfold what the Lord promised to those loving him.
>
> Then the wife reckoned the time of her husband's return, because if God permitted him to live, he would come home to her. He commended her to the Lord, kissed her, and promised as she wept that

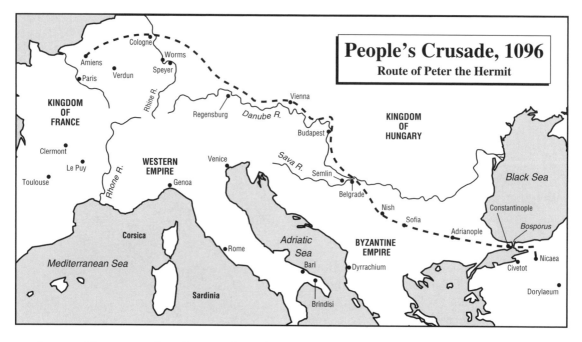

he would return. She, fearing that she would never see him again, not able to hold up, fell senseless to the ground; mourning her living beloved as if he were dead. He, having compassion, it seems, neither for the weeping of his wife, nor feeling pain for the grief of any friends, and yet having it, for he secretly suffered severely, unchanging, went away with a determined mind.

And so those men of determined mind went crusading—in the company of sadness, yes, but also filled with joy—for to a man they felt, "This is the Lord's doing; it is marvelous in our eyes."[62]

The People's Crusade

In the eyes of many unfortunate souls who lived along the several crusading routes to the East, the "Lord's doing" must have looked substantially less "marvelous." According to

Simon Lloyd, a leading Crusade scholar, Pope Urban II "had intended that the crusade army should consist fundamentally of knights and other ranks who would be militarily useful." But news of Urban's call to arms at Clermont spread rapidly throughout the West and he lost control of personnel recruitment.

Lloyd comments on some of the early "crusading" activity:

These bands, led by men like Peter the Hermit and Walter Sans-Avoir [the Penniless], were the first to depart, as early as spring 1096. Collectively, they are known traditionally as the People's Crusade, but in reality they were essentially independent groups of the poor, lacking supplies and equipment, though some contained or were even led by knights. Streaming from northern France, the Low Countries, the Rhineland, and Saxony in particular, they sought to reach Constantinople, but many failed to get even that far. Their foraging for food and lack of discipline, combined with their sheer ferocity, naturally alarmed the authorities in the lands through which they passed, above all the Byzantines. Many were killed in the inevitable armed clashes. Those who did get through to Constantinople were hurriedly shipped across the Bosporus in August 1096, after which they split into two groups. One attempted to take Nicaea but failed, the Turks surrounding and killing most; the other was ambushed and massacred near Civetot in August.

"The remnant," notes Lloyd, "fled back to Constantinople to join up with what has been identified as 'the second wave' of the crusade."[63]

By Land and Sea to Constantinople

Several contingents of troops were raised separately by a number of powerful princes, principally: Raymond of Toulouse; Godfrey of Bouillon and his brother, Baldwin of

A Remarkable Pile of Bones

In editor Elizabeth Hallam's *Chronicles of the Crusades*, Anna Comnena, daughter of Byzantine emperor Alexius I Comnenus, describes the amazement of her people at the sight of Peter the Hermit's "army" in Constantinople:

> To look upon them was like seeing rivers flowing together from all sides, and coming against us in full force, for the most part through Hungary. [Peter, ignoring the advice of Alexius to await the other Christian forces] crossed the [Strait of] Bosporus and pitched camp at a small village called Helenopolis, [where] as many as ten thousand French crusaders separated from the rest of the army. [They then] with the utmost cruelty, plundered the Turkish territory around Nicaea. They dismembered some of the babies, others they put on spits and roasted over a fire; those of advanced years they subjected to every form of torture.

In a violent clash with the defenders of Nicaea, the raiders forced their retreat and returned to Helenopolis with their booty. Upon learning of the pillaging at Nicaea and elsewhere, the Turkish sultan Qilij Arslan "placed men in ambush at suitable places" on the approaches to Nicaea. He then sent two messengers to the crusader camp to announce that some of Peter's followers

> had captured Nicaea and were dividing up the spoil from the city. . . . At the news of plunder and money, they immediately set off along the road to Nicaea, with no semblance of order, all forgetting their military skill and the discipline required of those going out to battle.

> . . . Since these men were advancing in no sort of order or discipline, they fell into the Turkish ambushes near Drakon and were miserably wiped out. Such a large number of Franks became the victims of Turkish swords, that when the scattered remains of the slaughtered men were collected, they made not merely a hill or mound or peak, but a huge mountain, deep and wide, most remarkable, so great was the pile of bones.

Boulogne; Robert of Normandy, his cousin, Robert of Flanders, and his brother-in-law, Stephen of Blois; and Hugh of Vermandois. Added to these were the Normans of southern Italy led by Bohemund of Taranto and his nephew Tancred.

"The real military forces took longer to assemble and organize," writes retired army colonel John F. Sloan, a faculty member of the U.S. Defense Intelligence College. "Beginning in March 1096 as individual knights and members of medieval hosts, they marched and sailed from throughout France and the Low Countries toward Constantinople, arriving there between December 1096 and May 1097."[64] Their journeys on the way to the Byzantine capital were anything but uneventful, as R. Ernest Dupuy and Trevor N. Dupuy illustrate:

Leaders of the First Crusade included (left to right) Godfrey, Raymond, Bohemund, and Tancred. The forces of these men made up the true military might of the Crusade.

Godfrey and Baldwin . . . followed the Danube Valley through Hungary, Serbia, and Bulgaria, thence over the Balkan mountains, having several armed brushes with local forces en route. Count Raymond and others from southern France proceeded through north Italy, continued down the barren Dalmatian coast to Durazzo in a grueling march, thence east to Constantinople.[65]

Hugh, the two Roberts, and Stephen led their contingents across the Alps and down the Italian peninsula. "Hugh of Vermandois . . . traveled by way of Rome to Bari, from where he set sail for Durazzo [Durres, Albania]," writes Jonathan Riley-Smith. "But a storm scattered his fleet and Hugh, who was forced to land some way from Durazzo, was briefly detained before being escorted to Constantinople."[66]

Robert of Flanders and his contingent, the next to arrive in Bari, crossed the Adriatic at once and reached Constantinople at about the same time as Bohemund. Robert of Normandy and Stephen of Blois arrived last in Bari. Facing heavy seas and the objections of local sailors, they decided to winter in southern Italy. On April 5, 1097, reports Fulcher of Chartres:

They boarded ship at the harbor of Brindisi on the eastern coast of Italy. Oh how deep and inscrutable are the decisions of God: for before our very eyes, one of the ships suddenly split in the middle, still close to the shore, for no apparent reason.

Four hundred men and women drowned. But all at once, joyous praise to God resounded: for when those who were standing around went to collect the corpses, the sign of the cross was found imprinted

The Hazards of Sea Travel

Whether traveling by land or by sea, crusaders faced many dangers en route to the Holy Land. In Anatomy of a Crusade 1213–1221, *James M. Powell, professor of history at Syracuse University, describes the hazards of sea travel during the Fifth Crusade:*

"Some three hundred ships departed from Vlerdingen in the Netherlands on May 29, 1217. This was the first contingent of the Fifth Crusade to actually get underway. It would not be the first to arrive in the East. . . .

The sea route chosen by the crusaders was perilous. There is no way to document fully how many of the ships that left Vlerdingen were lost at sea, but the number must have been substantial. Only a few days out, in the sea of Brittany, a ship from Monheim was wrecked on the rocks, and the fleet had to slow while its men were rescued from the rocks onto which they had climbed. Three more ships were wrecked in a storm off the Portuguese coast. Bishop James of Vitry, who had earlier travelled from Genoa to Acre, left a vivid description of the perils of travel on the treacherous waters of the Mediterranean. He described his fear during a storm in which the waters were breaking over his ship, and this was despite the fact that he was travelling on a newly constructed ship and the arrangements on board were well suited to his episcopal rank. . . . Still the trip was far from comfortable. Contrary winds impeded their progress. They ran into a storm of such magnitude that 'fifteen anchors could hardly hold the ship back' as the prow of the vessel rose to the stars and sank into the abyss. During the two days and nights that the storm lasted, many had nothing to eat, and James himself ate nothing cooked, because it was too dangerous to light a fire on the ship. Many on board took the opportunity to confess their sins and prepare for death. But finally the seas calmed and, with dolphins in their wake, they sailed toward Acre. Many travellers to the East were not so fortunate, however, and for them the crusade ended at sea."

in the flesh of some above the shoulder-blades.

Of the remainder who struggled with death, very few survived. The horses and mules were drowned and a great deal of money was lost.

We were confused and terrified by the sight of this misfortune, to the extent that many who were weak in heart and had not yet boarded ship returned home, giving up the journey, saying that they would never trust themselves again to the deceptive and treacherous sea. But we, putting our hope entirely in Almighty God, went to sea with foresails raised and trumpets blasting, wafted by a moderate breeze. Four days later we reached land, about ten miles, I would guess, from the city of Durazzo. Our fleet landed in two harbors and from there, with great joy, we continued on dry land and passed by Durazzo.[67]

The tribulations suffered by the armies of the First Crusade were experienced over and again by succeeding crusaders, who flowed to the Holy Land in an almost continuous flow of individuals and groups for the next two hundred years.

Death Along the Way

In 1188 Holy Roman Emperor Frederick Barbarossa took up the crusading cause as he approached the age of seventy. In May of the following year, he departed for Jerusalem with a large German army, a contingent of the Third Crusade. In a letter to his son Henry, written while en route to Constantinople, Frederick reported on the difficulties that he encountered along the way:

It seems worth reporting first that as soon as we reached the borders of the empire of our brother emperor of Constantinople, Isaac II Angelus, we sustained no little loss in the plundering of our property and in the massacre of our men, a loss reckoned to be clearly instigated by the emperor himself. [The alliance of Western and Eastern Christendom against the perceived Muslim threat was riddled with mutual dislike and distrust.] For some bandit archers, lurking in dense thorn bushes by the public highway, never ceased ambushing with their poisoned arrows several of our men who were unarmed and walking carelessly, until the bandits were completely surrounded by crossbows and by our knights; being caught red-handed they paid the price and met their just deserts. On a single day, thirty-two were strung up like outlaws and ended their lives miserably on a gibbet [an upright post with a projecting arm for hanging the bodies of executed criminals as a warning].

None the less, the remaining bandits harassed us from the mountain slopes throughout the whole wooded expanse of Bulgaria and molested us in night attacks even though a vast number of them were dreadfully tortured in turn by all kinds of devices by our army.

Frederick went on to write that Isaac II had "infringed every single agreement, sworn in his name and on his behalf by his chancellor" and by his threats had almost withdrawn from

Holy Roman Emperor Frederick Barbarossa stands in a ship during the Crusades. Seventy-year-old Frederick's journey was one of the most harrowing of the crusaders.

Frederick drowns while trying to cross the Calycadnus River. Without their leader, his army quickly disbanded.

them "the right to exchange and trade." And he told of several defenses—felled trees, great rocks, and refurbished fortifications—put in place against them by the Byzantine emperor, adding: "But we Germans, supported by heavenly aid, used Greek fire [a potent incendiary mixture, usually containing pitch, used to spread fire] and reduced the defenses and stonework to embers and ashes." Lastly, Frederick noted that after spending twelve weeks camped in Philippopolis, Bulgaria: "We have lost more than a hundred pilgrims who by dying have gone to the Lord. Many of our pilgrims from our empire are held captive in Constantinople."[68]

Frederick eventually patched up his problems with Isaac II and proceeded into Anatolia. He drowned en route to Antioch on June 10, 1190, trying to cross the shallow Calycadnus (Göksu) River. Leaderless, his army fell apart, thus contributing greatly to the failure of the Third Crusade.

With regard to Frederick's death, Ibn al-Athir, a thirteenth-century Muslim historian, writes: "If Allah had not deigned to show his benevolence toward the Muslims by having the king of the Germans perish . . . today we would be writing: Syria and Egypt formerly belonged to Islam."[69]

Of the inestimable thousands of knights and soldiers killed during the Crusades, experts can only speculate as to how many died somewhere along the way, never to reach the field of battle.

Sword and Scimitar: Battling for God and Allah

The armies of the First Crusade (1096–1099)—under the principal leaders Raymond of Toulouse, Robert of Normandy, and Godfrey of Bouillon—crossed Europe to Constantinople, assembling there in the spring of 1097. They proceeded across the Bosporus in May of that year and entered the domain of Kilij Arslan, Seljuk sultan of Rum. The crusaders first forced him to surrender Nicaea, his capital city, on June 19, after a siege of more than seven weeks. The anonymous author of *Gesta Francorum* (*Deeds of the Franks*), reputedly a follower of Bohemund of Taranto, paid tribute to the fighting qualities of the Turks:

> What man is so learned and wise that he can describe the prudence and warlike skill and courage of the Turks? Certainly if they had always been firm in Christianity and had been willing to confess the articles of our creed, no man would have found stronger or braver men, or more skilled in warfare; yet, by God's grace, our men had the upper hand.[70]

The crusaders next defeated Kilij Arslan's Turks at the Battle of Dorylaeum on July 1, 1097, thereby opening the route to Antioch. According to Peter the Monk, a scholarly French monk of St. Remy, Kilij Arslan attributed his defeat at Dorylaeum to men

> who do not fear death or the enemy. . . . Who could bear the sight of the splendor

A twelfth-century French depiction of the crusaders taking control of Nicaea, the capital of the Seljuk sultanate of Rum, in 1097.

of their terrifying arms? Their lances flashed like sparkling stars; their helmets and mailcoats like the glimmering light of a spring dawn. The clashing of their arms was more terrible than the sound of thunder. When they prepare themselves for battle they raise their lances high and then advance in ranks, as silently as though they are dumb [mute]. When they draw close to their adversaries then, loosing their reins, they charge with great force like lions which, spurred by hunger, thirst for blood. Then they shout and grind their teeth and fill the air with their cries. And they spare no one.[71]

The crusading armies then marched virtually unhindered across Asia Minor to Antioch. During a protracted siege at Antioch, from October 1097 to June 1098, the crusaders overcame the heat, treacherous terrain, and the fluid tactics of a nomadic enemy in learning how to defeat the Muslims.

The Fall of Jerusalem

On June 9, 1099, the crusaders reached Jerusalem and placed the city under siege. Godfrey of Bouillon had by then emerged as the principal leader. Five weeks later they assaulted the city in force. In *Gesta Francorum*, its anonymous author recounts the final onslaught like this:

> On Friday 15 July 1099, early in the morning, we attacked the city from all sides, but we could make no headway against it, and

we were all numb with astonishment and very frightened. Godfrey of Bouillon and his brother, Baldwin, count of Boulogne, were fighting bravely in the siege-tower. Then one of our knights, Lethold by name, climbed up on to the wall of the city. As soon as he had climbed it, all the defenders of the city fled along the walls and through the city, and our men, following Lethold, chased after them, killing and dismembering them as far as the Temple of Solomon. And in that place there was such a slaughter that we were up to our ankles in their blood.

Count Raymond of Toulouse and his forces stormed the city from the south, forcing the defenders to surrender and open the gate. The anonymous author continues:

> Our pilgrims entered the city, and chased the Saracens, killing as they went, as far as

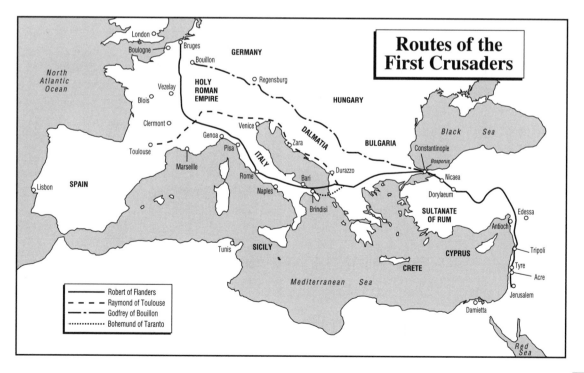

the Temple of Solomon. There the enemy assembled, and fought a furious battle for the whole day, so that their blood flowed all over the Temple. At last the pagans were overcome, and our men captured a good number of men and women in the Temple; they killed whomsoever they wished, and chose to keep others alive.

The conquering crusaders spent the remainder of the day "seizing gold and silver, horses and mules, and houses full of riches of all kinds." The nameless scribe finishes his account this way:

> In the morning our men climbed up cautiously on to the roof of the Temple and attacked the Saracens, both male and female, and beheaded them with unsheathed swords. The other Saracens threw themselves from the Temple.

> Then our men held a council, and gave out that everyone should give alms and pray that God would choose whom he wished to reign over the others and rule the city. They further gave orders that all the dead Saracens should be cast out on account of the terrible stench; because nearly the whole city was crammed with their bodies. The Saracens who were still alive dragged the dead ones out in front of the gates, and made huge piles of them, as big as houses. Such a slaughter of pagans no one has ever seen or heard of; the pyres they made were like pyramids.[72]

Eight days after the city's fall, the crusaders elected Godfrey of Bouillon as Guardian of Jerusalem. He declined the title of king. The First Crusade ended with the capture of Jerusalem and the establishment of the Crusader (or Latin) States in the Holy Land, which drew the attention of Europe for the next two hundred years.

The Second Crusade

A second expedition to the Holy Land—led by Conrad III, emperor of Germany, and Louis VII, king of France—failed to recapture territory lost to the Muslims after the First Crusade. The armies of the Second Crusade (1147–1149) set out for the Holy Land by separate routes. The Germans followed the same general route as the First Crusade; the French traveled a longer route, clinging to the coast to stay within Byzantine territory

After taking Jerusalem, Godfrey of Bouillon gives thanks at the Holy Sepulcher, considered the site of Jesus' tomb. The fall of Jerusalem ended the First Crusade.

A 1460 French depiction of Conrad III and Louis VII entering Constantinople during the Second Crusade.

as much as possible. Both armies engaged hostile forces and took severe losses along the way. By the time Conrad and Louis merged forces in Jerusalem in 1148, both had lost most of their troops.

Once united, the two kings decided to attack Damascus, the seizure of which would drive a wedge through Muslim territory. "The military idea was a good one," argues historian Henry Treece, "but the crusaders had neither the force required nor the friendship between Germans and French which would have made such a move possible."[73]

After besieging the city for only four days, the two kings withdrew their dispirited armies in the face of sporadic Muslim counterattacks. Sibt ibn al-Jauzi, a thirteenth-century Syrian historian, epitomizes the humiliating crusading reversals of the Second Crusade as follows:

The Franks had with them a great Priest with a long beard, whose teachings they obeyed. [During] the siege of Damascus

he mounted his ass, hung a cross around his neck, took two more in his hand and hung another round the ass's neck. He had the Testaments and the crosses and the Holy Scriptures set before him and assembled the army in his presence; the only ones to remain behind were those guarding the tents. Then he said: "The Messiah has promised me that today I shall wipe out this city." At this moment the Muslims opened the city gates and in the name of Islam charged as one man into the face of death. Never, in pagan times or since the coming of Islam, was there a day like this. One of the men of the Damascus militia reached the Priest, who was fighting in the front line, struck his head from his body and killed his ass too. As the whole Muslim army bore down upon them the Franks turned and fled. The Muslims killed 10,000, smote their cavalry with Greek fire, and pursued the army as far as the tents. Night separated them, and in the morning the

Franks were gone and no trace of them remained.[74]

Conrad III, a proud man, embarked immediately thereafter for Germany, shaken and disgusted; Louis VII returned to France a short time later. "The effect of this great movement was detrimental to the Frankish position in the Holy Land," writes military analyst John F. Sloan. "In addition, the fiasco so discredited the whole crusading idea that efforts to recruit a new force in 1150 failed."[75]

The Third Crusade

Following the loss of Jerusalem on October 2, 1187, and most of the Holy Land after the Battle of Hattin in July 1187, to the Muslim forces of Saladin, sultan of Egypt, a third campaign was mounted against the Muslims, principally headed by Richard I *Coeur de Lion* ("Lion's Heart," or Lionheart), king of England. The key events of the Third Crusade (1189–1192) were the two-year siege of Acre, the key seaport for Jerusalem; Richard's "fighting march" down the Mediterranean coastline to Jaffa, culminating "in an encounter outside Arsuf (7 September) in which Saladin's forces were routed";[76] and Richard's advance on Jerusalem.

Baha' ad-Din, who served with Saladin at Acre, later recorded his recollections of the sultan's courage in the face of Richard the Lionheart's assault on the seaside city in 1191:

> The Sultan, who learned of the assault from eye-witnesses and by an agreed signal from the garrison—a roll of drums—mounted his horse and ordered the army to mount and attack the enemy. A great battle was fought that day. As deeply concerned as a mother bereft of her child,

Richard the Lionheart led the Third Crusade against Saladin, but he died before he could retake Jerusalem.

> Saladin galloped from battalion to battalion inciting his men to fight for the Faith. . . . The Sultan moved through the ranks crying: "For Islam!" his eyes swimming with tears. Every time he looked toward Acre and saw the agony she was in and the disaster looming for her inhabitants, he launched himself once more into the attack and goaded his men on to fight. That day he touched no food and drank only a cup or two of the potion prescribed for him by his doctor. . . . Night fell, the Sultan returned to his tent after the final evening prayer, exhausted and in anguish, and slept fitfully. The next morning he had the drums beaten, marshalled his army and returned to the battle he had left the night before.[77]

Saladin's courageous attempts to save the city ended in failure. The Muslim garrison in Acre surrendered to Richard's crusaders on July 12, 1191.

Almost a year later, after months of marching and campaigning, Richard's forces moved resolutely toward Jerusalem. The *Itinerarium regis Ricardi*, a chronicle of Richard's crusading travels and experiences, describes his approach to the Holy City:

> On Friday 12 June 1192 a spy informed King Richard that some Turks were ambushing travellers in the hills. Early in the morning he set out from Beit Nuba [twelve miles from Jerusalem] to find them, and surprised them at dawn by the spring of Emmaeus. In the attack twenty Turks were taken and the rest scattered. The only prisoner to be spared was Saladin's personal herald, whose duty it was to announce his decrees. Three camels, horses, mules and some fine Turkomans [Turkic-speaking people of central Asia] were captured. The king also obtained two good mules laden with precious silk garments, as well as many kinds of spices, including aloes.
>
> Richard hunted the Saracens closely as they fled through the hills, killing as he went. Pursuing one of them into a valley, he had just unhorsed him, pierced and dying, and was crushing him underfoot when he looked up. There, afar off, the city of Jerusalem appeared before his eyes.[78]

Richard the Lionheart never reached Jerusalem. On September 2, 1192, Richard, weary and by then losing interest in the campaign, agreed to a treaty with Saladin. "I will return in three years to conquer the Holy Land," Richard wrote to the sultan. Saladin replied: "If I must lose the Holy Land, there is no one to whom I would rather lose it than the English king."[79]

The Third Crusade failed to recapture Jerusalem. But it restored the military balance to the Franks and for that it was considered successful.

The Fourth Crusade

In 1198 Pope Innocent III raised a crusade in France, hoping to attack the seat of Muslim power in Egypt. But he lost control of the expedition. Through a series of political machinations by crusading leaders to install a Latin ruler in Constantinople, the Fourth Crusade (1202–1204) ended in tragedy. Elizabeth Hallam, acclaimed scholar of medieval history, writes:

Saladin, leader of the Muslim army, gained great respect for Richard the Lionheart.

In 1204 the army of the Fourth Crusade attacked and sacked Constantinople, capital of the Byzantine Empire, seat of the patriarch of the eastern church, and treasure-house of a magnificent heritage, cultural, artistic, and intellectual, that stretched back to the heyday of the Roman Empire.[80]

Robert of Clari, a humble knight and noted chronicler of the Fourth Crusade, described the booty that awaited the conquerors of Constantinople:

There was so much treasure heaped up there, so many precious gold and silver vessels, cloth of gold and rich jewels, that it was a wonder to behold. Never since the beginning of the world has such wealth been seen or been won—not in Charlemagne's day, nor even in Alexander's. I do not think that in the forty rich-

est cities in the world you could find such treasure as we found in Constantinople. The Greeks used to say that two-thirds of the world's wealth was concentrated in Constantinople and the other third scattered throughout the rest of the world.[81]

Crusading leaders commandeered innumerable Byzantine palaces that also contained great treasures, such as the palace of Boukoleon, occupied by Boniface, marquis of Montferrat and commander of the victorious army. Shortly after the city fell to the crusaders, Baldwin, the first Latin emperor of Constantinople, rewarded the marquis by granting the land of Salonika to him. But the marquis enjoyed his new wealth and prominence for only three years.

In 1207 Boniface, while returning from Adrianople with a small party of knights, was ambushed by a band of Bulgarians. As reported by Geoffrey of Villehardouin, a cru-

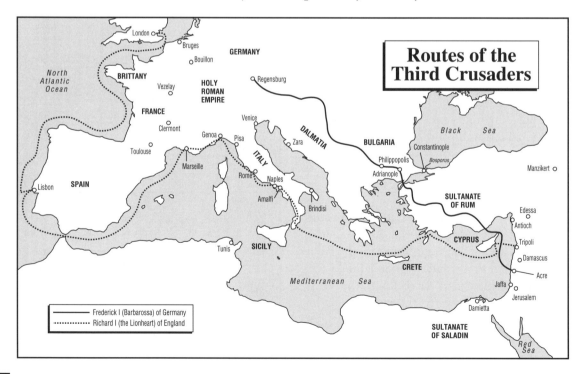

Routes of the Third Crusaders

— Frederick I (Barbarossa) of Germany
····· Richard I (the Lionheart) of England

sading leader and loyal subordinate of the marquis, upon hearing his rear guard raise a cry of alarm, Boniface

leapt on his horse, all unarmed as he was, with only a lance in his hand. When he reached the place where the Bulgarians were at grips with the rear-guard, he charged right in amongst them, and drove them back a good way.

As he flew after them, the marquis was fatally wounded in the thick of the arm, below the shoulder blade, and began to lose blood. When his men saw what had happened, their courage began to ebb, they lost their heart and started to give way.

Those who were nearest to the marquis held him up; he was losing so much blood that he began to faint. Realizing that they could expect no further help from their leader, his men gave way to panic and began to desert him. So, by an unlucky chance, they were defeated. Those who remained with the marquis—and there were very few—were killed. The Bulgarians cut off the marquis's head and sent it to Johanitza. That was one of the greatest joys the King of Wallachia [a region in south Romania] had ever experienced.[82]

As a result of the Fourth Crusade, the crusading movement moved further away from spiritual motivation and church control and

Joinville's Priest

Except during the First and Third Crusades, the crusaders failed in achieving most of their objectives. But their failures resulted not through a lack of valor. In Chronicles of the Crusades, *edited by Elizabeth Hallam, Jean de Joinville, a French nobleman who participated in the Seventh Crusade, recounts the following example of individual heroism. Under a shower of arrows from eight of the Saracens' leading officers, one of Joinville's priests left camp alone and*

"advanced towards the Saracens, trailing his spear behind him under his arm, with the point towards the ground, so the Saracens should not catch sight of it.

When he came near the Saracens, who scorned him because they saw he was all alone, he quickly drew his spear from under his arm and ran at them. Not a single one of the eight thought of defending himself, but all turned and fled. When the Saracens on

horseback saw their lords flying towards them, they spurred forward to rescue them, while at the same time some fifty of our sergeants came rushing out of camp. The mounted Saracens continued to urge on their horses, but not daring to attack our footmen, they suddenly swerved aside.

After they had done this two or three times, one of our sergeants grasped his lance by the middle and hurled it at one of the Turks, so that it stuck him between the ribs. The wounded man turned back with the lance hanging by its head from his body. On seeing this the Turks no longer dared to advance, and retreated before us. . . . From that time onwards my priest was very well known throughout the army, and one man or another would point him out and say: 'Look, that's my Lord of Joinville's priest, who got the better of eight Saracens.'"

In a bizarre turn of events, the crusaders, who have pledged to uphold Christianity, ransack and loot Constantinople, the seat of Christianity in the East.

more toward political and economical stimuli and state control. The sacking of Constantinople effectively marked the end of Byzantine dominance in the East. But the Franks' rule in Constantinople was neither long nor happy.

"The simple-minded, bluff European stood no more chance of survival there than he had done earlier in the wind-blown waste of Syria," attests Henry Treece, master narrator of the Crusades. "By 1261 the crusaders had become so decadent that the ever-surging primitives about them, the Bulgarians and Serbs, the Wallachians and the Greeks, beat them out of Constantinople like figures of mockery in an old play."[83]

Blade of the Victor

Four more crusades followed over the next sixty-eight years and are generally considered to have fallen short of their objectives. Most historians regard only the First and Third Crusades as having been successes, and the latter only moderately so. Comments Will Durant, "The power and prestige of the Roman Church were immensely enhanced by the First Crusade, and progressively damaged by the rest."[84] Ultimately, when the clank and clang of sword against scimitar echoed for the last time across the Holy Land, it was the curved blade of Islam that was sheathed in victory.

The Crusader States: Christian Life in the Shadow of Islam

After the First Crusade, most of the crusaders returned home. But a few remained in the Holy Land to establish Christian colonies, namely, Baldwin in the County of Edessa, Bohemund in the principality of Antioch, Raymond in the county of Tripoli, and Godfrey in the kingdom of Jerusalem. Technically, the Greek emperor, to whom the crusaders had pledged their allegiance in Constantinople, ruled over Jerusalem, and Jerusalem held nominal feudal authority over the other three Latin states. In reality, however, the crusaders disavowed their pledges to the Byzantine ruler and pledged themselves anew to the pope in Rome. Moreover, the four Latin states operated more as a loose confederation than as a unified sovereignty ruled by the king of Jerusalem.

A Powerful Coalition

These colonies became known as the Crusader (or Latin) States. "With Muslim Syria divided among its many factions, the four Latin states—Jerusalem, Antioch, Edessa, and Tripoli—formed a powerful, if fragile, coalition," writes French historian Georges Tate, a specialist in the history of the East from the third century B.C. to the twelfth century A.D. "Their strength came from the solidity of their political institutions, which conferred a large measure of authority on the

king or prince." This colonizing effort by the Western invaders surprised the vanquished Muslims, as noted by Georges Tate:

> For the Muslims the loss of Jerusalem had been a religious defeat, but not a great disaster. They assumed that, like other invaders, the Franks would either eventually move on or gradually assimilate. To the surprise of the Muslims and Eastern Christians, the Franks were not

Godfrey remained in the Holy Land and established a Christian colony in Jerusalem.

like other invaders. They sought to dominate the people they had defeated. They distinguished between victor and vanquished, Frank and non-Frank, on the basis of origin and religion. There was no solidarity between the crusaders who settled in the East and the native populations. The Franks—Roman Catholic and originally from Europe— clustered in the cities. Periodic waves of immigration increased their numbers, but they remained a minority, separated from the rest of the people by a huge rift.[85]

Establishing the Crusader States

Edessa became the first of the four Latin states established in the East as a result of the First Crusade. Baldwin of Boulogne left the crusading army at Konya in Asia Minor, in October 1097 and proceeded east into Cilicia in search of land and booty. When he reached Edessa, then ruled by the unpopular Prince Thoros, a Byzantine subject, Baldwin allegedly conspired to overthrow the prince. "Baldwin discovered evil counsellors in Edessa, traitors who plotted with him to have Thoros killed and promised to hand Edessa over to him," writes Matthew of Edessa, an Armenian chronicler. "Baldwin agreed to join them."[86]

According to Albert of Aachen, Thoros tried to escape from his would-be usurpers, but they "immediately shot him down in the middle of the street, with a thousand arrows. And cutting off his head, they carried it fixed on a spear through all the quarters of the city for everyone to mock."[87] Baldwin readily succeeded Thoros and became Prince Baldwin of Edessa.

The principality of Antioch became the second Crusader State in 1098. "The grim

siege [of Antioch] lasted seven months and was ended with typical Norman ruthlessness and craft by Bohemond; who got in touch with Firuz, one of the besieged Turkish emirs known to be tired of the whole affair," writes Henry Treece. "He was promised all safety and honors if he would betray the city."[88] But Bohemund stipulated that the emir's safety was contingent upon himself being made prince of that city when it fell.

The emir did his job. "The tower which he commanded overlooked the valley; its gates were opened, and a large number of Franks managed to get in by using ropes," reported Arab historian Ibn al-Athir about a century later. In the subsequent confusion, one of the city gates was opened inadvertently. "The Frankish army entered through the open gate, ransacked the town and killed any Muslims that they came across."[89] After several months

Baldwin of Boulogne (on horseback) ruled the Latin state of Edessa after overthrowing Prince Thoros.

After a seven-month-long siege, crusaders storm Antioch, ransacking the town and slaying its Muslim inhabitants.

mountain villages of Lebanon to this day," writes crusading authority Malcolm Billings. "The Assassins [or Hashishiyun, a Muslim Shiite sect renown as political assassins] were also neighbors of the Franks in Syria."[91] Originally from Persia (Iran), the Assassins established themselves in a group of castles east of Antioch and Tripoli during the early 1100s.

Lastly, the kingdom of Jerusalem was founded on Friday, July 15, 1099. It stretched from just north of Beirut and extended southward along the coast to just south of Gaza. A string of castles along the edge of the desert—encompassing Palestine and continuing as far south as the Red Sea—marked its eastern boundary. "On the eighth day after the city was captured, [the crusaders] chose Godfrey of Bouillon as ruler of the city [advocate of the Holy Sepulcher and Guardian of Jerusalem], to subdue the pagans and protect the Christians," scribed Fulcher of Chartres. "So too they chose as patriarch that wise and noble man by the name of Arnulf, on 1 August 1099."[92] Godfrey reigned for only a year before he died, probably of disease. He lived just long enough to ensure the survival of the infant Christian state. His brother, Baldwin, count of Edessa, succeeded him and was crowned Baldwin I, the first king of Jerusalem.

Unique in Its Time

The new kingdom of Jerusalem was unique in its time, its makeup and government, its population mix, and the way its people lived. Malcolm Billings, a scholar of the crusading phenomenon, explains how Jerusalem partially governed and otherwise interacted with the other three Latin states:

> The fledgling crusader states [the leaders of the First Crusade] founded were a

of haggling with Raymond of Toulouse for possession and control of Antioch, "Bohemond," in the words of Will Durant, "became by grateful consent Prince of Antioch."[90]

Immediately to the south of Antioch, in a narrow strip of land between Mount Lebanon and the coast, Raymond of Toulouse founded the county of Tripoli. "Southern French made up the bulk of the European settlers who ruled a mainly Muslim population; among the Christian minorities were the Maronites [Syrian Christians] who have maintained their identity in the

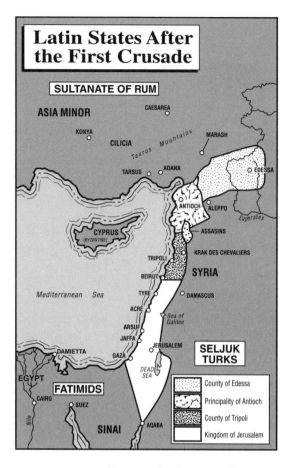

Latin States After the First Crusade

SULTANATE OF RUM

ASIA MINOR

CAESAREA

KONYA

CILICIA

Taurus Mountains

MARASH

TARSUS

ADANA

EDESSA

ANTIOCH

ALEPPO

Euphrates

CYPRUS
(BYZANTINE)

ASSASSINS

TRIPOLI

KRAK DES CHEVALIERS

BEIRUT

SYRIA

TYRE

DAMASCUS

Mediterranean Sea

ACRE

Sea of Galilee

ARSUF

JAFFA

JERUSALEM

DAMIETTA

GAZA

SELJUK TURKS

EGYPT

DEAD SEA

CAIRO

FATIMIDS

SUEZ

Nile

SINAI

AQABA

County of Edessa

Principality of Antioch

County of Tripoli

Kingdom of Jerusalem

crusader states governed themselves, and pursued foreign policies that suited their regional aspirations at the time. The King and the ruling lords devolved the administration still further by granting large tracts of land and towns or castles to fief holders who were given a free hand in the way they ran their lordships.[93]

With respect to the multicultural populace in the Latin East, over which the Christian conquerors seized control, Jonathan Phillips, a historian of that era, comments:

> The settlers [crusaders] had conquered an area inhabited by a bewildering variety of races and creeds. There was a native Jewish population; Druzes; Zoroastrians; Christians such as Armenians, Maronites, Jacobites, and Nestorians, together with a sizeable Greek Orthodox community. There were also Muslims: both Sunni and Shi'i. Some Europeans were familiar with the eastern Mediterranean [not] on account of pilgrimage and commerce[,] but because the crusaders wanted to capture and settle the Holy Land[,] the relationship between the Franks and the indigenous population was very different to that in any of their previous encounters.

> An important element in the process of settlement was the Latins' treatment of the native inhabitants. The early years of the conquest were marked by a series of massacres, probably as a result of a policy whereby sites of religious or strategic significance were to be reserved to Christians. But it soon became apparent that this was counterproductive.

The crusaders found themselves in a situation in which they had acquired so much territory

potpourri of race and religion and to govern them the crusader lords superimposed the sort of feudal society they were familiar with in the West, with the Crown [Jerusalem] presiding over a collection of quasi-independent fiefs: Antioch was legally separate because technically it was a vassal state of the [Byzantine] Empire; the counts of Tripoli and Edessa were personally vassals of the Kings of Jerusalem but otherwise their counties were semi-independent; the crusader lords of Palestine were obliged to render military service to the King of Jerusalem and accept his judgements, handed down by the High Court, which was composed of his chief vassals. But by and large the

Baldwin I Arranges His Own Funeral

Baldwin I, the first king of Jerusalem, contracted a fatal disease during a raid against the Fatimid caliphate in Egypt in 1118. In *Historia Hierosolymitana*, twelfth-century Christian historian Albert of Aachen writes about Baldwin's last requests (as excerpted in Elizabeth Hallam's *Chronicles of the Crusades*):

> Baldwin told all who were present, very insistently and appealing to their good faith, that if he died, they should never bury his body in any grave in the land of the Saracens, lest it be held in derision and mockery by the infidels, but with all the skill and exertion they could muster, they should carry his corpse back to Jerusalem, and bury it next to his brother Godfrey of Bouillon.

His followers protested that it would be impossible to preserve his corpse in the summer heat, whereupon he instructed them:

> "As soon as I die, I entreat you to open my stomach with a knife, embalm my body with salt and spices and wrap it in a skin or hangings, and in this way it may be taken back to a Christian funeral in Jerusalem and buried next to my brother's grave."
>
> Without delay he summoned Addo the cook, who was one of the household, and he bound him with an oath concerning the cutting of his stomach and the throwing-out of his internal organs. He also said to him: 'You know that I am shortly to die. On this subject, as you love me, or as you used to love me when I was alive and well, so should you keep faith with me when I am dead. Disembowel me with the knife; rub me inside and outside especially with salt; fill my eyes, nostrils, ears and mouth generously; and be sure to take me back with the rest. In this way know that you are fulfilling my wishes, and believe you are keeping faith with me in this matter.' And so it was arranged.

Surrounded by his faithful troops, Baldwin lies on his deathbed after returning from Egypt.

that they "lacked sufficient manpower to rebuild and defend urban communities. In consequence their approach to the local population changed."[94]

A twelfth-century Muslim writer, apparently impressed by the way Christians dealt with those of other religions when he was traveling through Palestine, writes, "We passed through a series of villages and cultivated lands all inhabited by Muslims, who live in great well-being under the Franks." He noted that they were paying less tax under the Christians than they had before. "One of the chief tragedies of the Muslims is that they have to complain of injustices of their own rulers, whereas they cannot but praise the behavior of the Franks, their natural enemies. May Allah soon put an end to this state of affairs!"[95]

Christians in the Crusader States

Insofar as Christian life in the Crusader States is concerned, it is perhaps no overstatement to say that few can improve on Henry Treece's terse commentary on how the mystical qualities of the Latin East must have appeared to newcomers from the West, "many of them still boys":

> The towns of the Holy Lands must have seemed incomparably beautiful: white houses, decked with laurels and vines, their doors and windows protected by striped awnings, standing along the steep and narrow roads; and where roads met, cool fountains playing, and white doves hovering in the sunlight; turbaned and bearded Armenians speaking with naked black Africans; olive-faced Greeks or Venetians arguing with sallow Arab or yellow-haired men from the far north. . . .

Within the houses would be pillows and divans stuffed with fine down for the travellers to recline upon. The floors would be of brightly colored mosaic; the dishes of wrought copper; there would be ivory boxes carved as delicately as lace, containing preserved fruits, almond paste and fragrant spices. And always there would be quietly smiling women dressed in fine muslin, their arms and legs jingling with bracelets of gold, silver and burnished copper.

Nor would newcomers lack for medicinal aid in times of sickness or injury or after too many sips of the grape:

> Even the medicines for the sick had about them the air of magic—potions containing opium and powdered gold, pastes of rose-jelly and spiced cream for delicate stomachs—so different from the crude northern "remedies" the crusaders had known: tinctures drawn from earthworms; poultices of adder's flesh, pounded together with wood-lice and spiders; broth compounded of human brains, oil, wine, and ants' eggs.[96]

For those adventurers from the West who proved incapable of coping with the extravagances and temptations of the East, and there were many, the mesmerizing mystique of the East worked in adverse ways:

> The average European adapted himself quickly to the rich and civilized life of Jerusalem without regrets. Quickly he learned to smoke opium, and to make use of the Negro slaves who were so easily procurable from Genoese and Venetian shipment. Any crusader who had spent more than five years abroad tended to

The Lion and the Ox

After the Crusader States were established in the Holy Land, Fulcher of Chartres wrote about "The Latins in the Levant" in Book III of his Chronicles. *The following account of Fulcher is extracted, in part, from Edward Peters's* The First Crusade:

"Consider, I pray, and reflect how in our time God has transferred the West into the East. For we who were Occidentals now have been made Orientals. He who was a Roman or a Frank is now a Galilaean, or an inhabitant of Palestine. One who was a citizen of Rheims or Chartres now has been made a citizen of Tyre or of Antioch. We have already forgotten the places of our birth; already they have become unknown to many of us, or, at least, are unmentioned.

Some already possess here homes and servants which they have received through inheritance. Some have taken wives not merely of their own people, but Syrians, or Armenians, or even Saracens who have received the grace of baptism. Some have with them father-in-law, or daughter-in-law, or son-in-law, or step-son, or step-father. There are here, too, grandchildren and great-grandchildren. One cultivates vines, another the fields. The one and the other use mutually the speech and the idioms of the different language. Different languages, now made common, become known to both races, and faith unites those whose forefathers were strangers. As it is written, 'The lion and the ox shall eat straw together.'"

speak Arabic with a fair accuracy and to think of new arrivals from Europe as "foreigners." No longer did one cause, or one leader, excite his interest. Indeed, surrounded by a wealth of luxuries he had never known before, and in a climate that seemed to absolve the average European from violent action, he soon lost all desire to serve any cause or master whose needs were different from his own.

Concludes Treece: "Out of such luxury inevitably grew disunity of purpose."[97] And disunity of purpose fostered a complacency among the crusaders that ultimately enabled the Muslims to wrest back the lands that had for centuries belonged to Islam.

In order to secure and sustain the Crusader States in the East, it was essential to control some 625 miles of coastline along the eastern shores of the Mediterranean Sea, the area known as the Levant. To do so, the major Levantine ports had to be captured and fortified, along with other inland areas. This, of course, led to more fighting and spawned the development of a system of crusader castles. According to R. C. Smail, a noted historian of crusading warfare, the Frankish colonists occupied existing castles and

> new castles were built in those areas into which it was desired to carry the Latin dominion and in those in which force was particularly required to support the work of administration or exploitation. It is easy to see that there was a military element in such use of fortified buildings, but it was fused with administrative, economic, and social considerations.

The walled town and castle are seen most clearly as military instruments during the

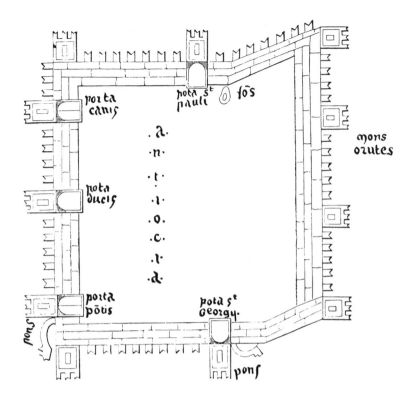

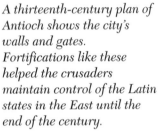

A thirteenth-century plan of Antioch shows the city's walls and gates. Fortifications like these helped the crusaders maintain control of the Latin states in the East until the end of the century.

crusaders' conquest and settlement in Syria, and during the great Muslim counter-attacks on the Latin states. When the Franks were the invaders, the castle was used as an offensive weapon. When they themselves were invaded, the castles were the final refuge of their authority.[98]

The fall of Acre in 1291 marked the end of the Christian dominions in the East. Dur-ing the next century, according to military historians R. Ernest Dupuy and Trevor N. Dupuy, "the crusading spirit died a lingering death."[99] Crusading movements of one kind or another continued for several centuries. Some modern historians view the Crusades as extending over seven centuries in many theaters of war. But the interest of most historians fades abruptly with the conclusion of the numbered crusades in 1272.

The Crusading Spirit and the March of Civilization

Will Durant described the Crusades as "the culminating act of the medieval drama, and perhaps the most picturesque event in the history of Europe and the Near East." Few students of that era would disagree. At the same time, most historians speak with a single voice in pronouncing the Crusades a failure. Durant himself opines:

Of their direct and professed purposes the Crusades had failed. After two centuries of war, Jerusalem was in the hands of the ferocious Mamluks [Egyptians], and Christian pilgrims came fewer and more fearful than before. The Moslem powers, once tolerant of religious diversity, had been made intolerant by attack. The Palestinian and Syrian ports that had been captured for Italian trade were without exception lost. Moslem civilization had proved itself superior to the Christian in refinement, comfort, education, and war.[100]

Feudalism recovered but with great difficulty. Both the western and eastern Roman Empires were severely weakened; the regime in Constantinople never regained its former power or stature. The Christian Church and its leaders suffered enormous losses in prestige and influence. Nor did Islam escape the deleterious effects of the Crusades, for it also

Christians return home after the First Crusade. Over time the territory won during the hard fought battles was taken from the crusaders.

suffered an erosion of strength and later fell victim to the Mongol flood from the East.

"A Long Act of Intolerance"

Through two centuries of Holy Wars, the soldiers of Christ won many battles but overall lost the wars. Steven Runciman, perhaps the dean of modern-day historians of the Crusades, ends his three-volume history with a high degree of moral indignation:

The triumphs of the Crusades were the triumphs of faith. But faith without wisdom is a dangerous thing. . . . In the long sequence of interaction and fusion between Orient and Occident out of which our civilization has grown, the Crusades were a tragic and destructive episode. . . .

A Crusader Laments Leaving His Love

To have perfect joy in paradise
I must leave the land I love so much,
Where she lives whom I thank every
    day.
Her body is noble and spirited, her
    face fresh and lovely;
And my true heart surrenders all to
    her.
But my body must take its leave of her;
I am departing for the place where
    God suffered death
To ransom us on a Friday.

Sweet love, I have a great sorrow in my
    heart
Now that at last I must leave you,
With whom I have found so much
    good, such tenderness,
Joy and gaiety to charm me.
But fortune by her power has made
    me
Exchange my joy for the sadness and
    sorrow
I will feel for many nights and many
    days.
Thus will I go to serve my creator.

No more than a child can endure
    hunger—
And no one can chastise him for crying
    because of it—

Do I believe that I can stay away
From you, whom I used to kiss and to
    embrace,
Nor have I in me such power of abstinence.
A hundred times a night I shall recall
    your beauty:
It gave me such pleasure to hold your
    body!
When I no longer have it I shall die of
    desire.

Good Lord God, if I for you
Leave the country where she is that I
    love so,
Grant us in heaven everlasting joy,
My love and me, through your mercy,
And grant her the strength to love me,
So that she will not forget me in my
    long absence,
For I love her more than anything in
    the world
And I feel so sad about her that my
    heart is breaking.

From a translation by Louise Riley-Smith in *The Crusades: Documents of Medieval History*. Reprinted in Malcolm Billings, *The Crusades: Five Centuries of Holy Wars*.

There was so much courage and so little honor, so much devotion and so little understanding. High ideals were besmirched by cruelty and greed, enterprise and endurance by a blind and narrow self-righteousness; and the Holy War itself was nothing more than a long act of intolerance in the name of God, which in itself is a sin against the Holy Ghost.[101]

In fairness to most crusaders it should be remembered, however, that their actions were initiated in the firm, unquestioned belief that "God wills it!"

Whether motivated by God or by greed, the impact of the Crusades on the individual crusader, his family and friends, and his tenants, was devastating. Historian Simon Lloyd submits that

> it was at this very personal and human level that the crusading movement wrought perhaps its most powerful and poignant influence for those caught up within it at the time. As in all wars, many participants returned physically or mentally scarred, if they returned at all; their lives could never be the same again. Nor could the lives of crusaders' wives and children, and those otherwise entwined in the crusader's fate for one reason or another. Modern historical research is only now beginning to unearth the profundities of the crusading movement's impact at this fundamental level.[102]

There were, of course, some mitigating consequences emanating from the Crusades.

"Next to the weakening of Christian belief, the chief effect of the Crusades was to stimulate the secular life of Europe by acquaintance with Moslem commerce and industry," surmises Will Durant. "War does one good—it teaches people geography."[103]

Renewal

"Although the crusading movement died out in northern Europe, some of its ideas found fertile soil in the New World," asserts Elizabeth Hallam, who goes on to explain:

> Monarchs who financed the voyages of discovery, and the men who undertook them, were strongly influenced by the goals which had characterized the crusading movement. . . .
>
> If modern historians of the crusades find it increasingly difficult to say when the movement drew to a close, it is because its attributes and features can be detected in so many areas of activity and thought in the 16th century and later, in the Old World and the New.[104]

"The Crusades had begun with an agricultural feudalism inspired by German barbarism crossed with religious sentiment," concludes Will Durant. "They ended with the rise of industry, and the expansion of commerce, in an economic revolution that heralded and financed the Renaissance."[105] And civilization marched on from there in the clearer light of renewed awakening.

Notes

Introduction: For God and Glory

1. Robert Payne, *The Dream and the Tomb: A History of the Crusades.* Chelsea, MI: Scarborough House, 1991, p. 27.
2. Quoted in Payne, *The Dream and the Tomb,* pp. 28–29.
3. André Corvisier, "Holy War," in André Corvisier and John Childs, eds., *A Dictionary of Military History.* Trans. Chris Turner. Cambridge, MA: Blackwell Publishers, 1994, p. 359.
4. Corvisier, "Holy War," in Corvisier and Childs, eds., *A Dictionary of Military History,* p. 359.
5. Corvisier, "Holy War," in Corvisier and Childs, eds., *A Dictionary of Military History,* p. 360.
6. Edward Peters, "Introduction," in Edward Peters, ed., *The First Crusade: The Chronicle of Fulcher of Chartres and Other Source Materials.* Philadelphia: University of Pennsylvania Press, 1971, p. xv.
7. Marcus Bull, "Origins," in Jonathan Riley-Smith, ed., *The Oxford Illustrated History of the Crusades.* New York: Oxford University Press, 1995, p. 16.
8. Jonathan Riley-Smith, "The Crusading Movement and Historians," in *The Oxford Illustrated History of the Crusades,* p. 1.
9. Payne, *The Dream and the Tomb,* p. 32.
10. Quoted in Will Durant, *The Age of Faith: A History of Medieval Civilization—Christian, Islamic, and Judaic—from Constantine to Dante: A.D. 325–1300.* Vol. 4 of *The Story of Civilization.* New York: Simon and Schuster, 1950, p. 587.

Chapter 1: Life in the Christian West

11. Sherrilyn Kenyon, *The Writer's Guide to Everyday Life in the Middle Ages: The British Isles from 500 to 1500.* Cincinnati: Writer's Digest Books, 1995, pp. 160–61.
12. Durant, *The Age of Faith,* pp. 553–54.
13. Durant, *The Age of Faith,* p. 579.
14. James Harpur, with Elizabeth Hallam, consultant, *Revelations: The Medieval World.* New York: Henry Holt, 1995, pp. 54–55.
15. Peter Draper, "The Architectural Setting of Gothic Art," in Nigel Saul, ed., *Age of Chivalry: Art and Society in Late Medieval England.* London: Brockhampton Press, 1995, pp. 62, 64.
16. Philip Warner, *The Medieval Castle.* New York: Barnes & Noble, 1993, pp. 189, 192.
17. Joseph and Frances Gies, *Life in a Medieval Castle.* New York: Harper & Row, 1974, pp. 116–17.
18. Kenyon, *The Writer's Guide to Everyday Life in the Middle Ages,* pp. 12–13.
19. Kenyon, *The Writer's Guide to Everyday Life in the Middle Ages,* p. 15.
20. Durant, *The Age of Faith,* p. 558.
21. "Middle Ages—The Peasant's Life," in *Compton's Interactive Encyclopedia,* version 3.00, Compton's New Media, 1995.
22. Kenyon, *The Writer's Guide to Everyday Life in the Middle Ages,* p. 19.
23. Durant, *The Age of Faith,* p. 559.

Chapter 2: Soldiers of the Cross

24. Frances Gies, *The Knight in History*. New York: Harper & Row, 1987, pp. 2–3.
25. Durant, *The Age of Faith*, p. 572.
26. Ebenezer Cobham Brewer, *Dictionary of Phrase and Fable*, 14th ed., Ivor H. Evans, ed. New York: Harper & Row, 1989, p. 392.
27. Quoted in A. V. B. Norman, *The Medieval Soldier*. New York: Barnes & Noble, 1993, pp. 151–52.
28. Gies and Gies, *Life in a Medieval Castle*, p. 115.
29. Quoted in Hans Delbrück, *Medieval Warfare*. Vol. 3 of *History of the Art of Warfare*. Trans. Walter J. Renfroe Jr. Lincoln: University of Nebraska Press, 1990, p. 241.
30. Nicholas Hooper and Matthew Bennett, *The Cambridge Illustrated Atlas of Warfare: The Middle Ages 768–1487*. New York: Cambridge University Press, 1996, p. 155.
31. Durant, *The Age of Faith*, pp. 572–73.
32. Harpur, *Revelations*, p. 38.
33. Michael Prestwich, *Armies and Warfare in the Middle Ages: The English Experience*. New Haven, CT: Yale University Press, 1996, p. 227.
34. Quoted in Gies, *The Knight in History*, p. 206.
35. Hooper and Bennett, *The Cambridge Illustrated Atlas of Warfare*, p. 156.
36. Quoted in Hooper and Bennett, *The Cambridge Illustrated Atlas of Warfare*, p. 156.
37. Quoted in Hooper and Bennett, *The Cambridge Illustrated Atlas of Warfare*, p. 156.
38. Bernard S. Bachrach, "On Roman Ramparts," in Geoffrey Parker, ed., *The Cambridge Illustrated History of Warfare*. New York: Cambridge University Press, 1995, pp. 88, 90–91.

Chapter 3: Life in the Muslim East

39. Durant, *The Age of Faith*, pp. 341–42.
40. Georges Tate, *The Crusaders: Warriors of God*. Trans. Lory Frankel. New York: Harry N. Abrams, 1996, p. 16.
41. John Alden Williams, ed., *Islam*. Vol. 5 of *Great Religions of Modern Man*. New York: George Braziller, 1962, p. 132.
42. Quoted in Williams, *Islam*, p. 121.
43. Durant, *The Age of Faith*, p. 222.
44. Durant, *The Age of Faith*, p. 222.
45. Basim Musallam, "The Ordering of Muslim Societies," in Francis Robinson, ed., *The Cambridge Illustrated History of the Islamic World*. Cambridge, UK: Cambridge University Press, 1996, p. 165.
46. Musallam, "The Ordering of Muslim Societies," in Robinson, ed., *The Cambridge Illustrated History of the Islamic World*, p. 169.
47. Musallam, "The Ordering of Muslim Societies," in Robinson, ed., *The Cambridge Illustrated History of the Islamic World*, p. 169.
48. Williams, *Islam*, p. 130.
49. Durant, *The Age of Faith*, p. 224.
50. Quoted in Williams, *Islam*, p. 125.
51. Durant, *The Age of Faith*, p. 223.
52. Quoted in Williams, *Islam*, p. 99.

Chapter 4: Warriors of the Crescent

53. Delbrück, *Medieval Warfare*, pp. 210–11.
54. R. Ernest Dupuy and Trevor N. Dupuy, *The Encyclopedia of Military History*, rev. ed. New York: Harper & Row, 1977, pp. 199–200.

55. Dupuy and Dupuy, *The Encyclopedia of Military History*, p. 200.

56. John Matthews and Bob Stewart, *Warriors of Christendom: Charlemagne, El Cid, Barbarossa, Richard Lionheart*. Poole, UK: Firebird Books, 1988, pp. 58–59.

57. Matthews and Stewart, *Warriors of Christendom*, p. 59.

58. Lawrence D. Higgins, "Arab Tactics," in Franklin D. Margiotta, ed., *Brassey's Encyclopedia of Military History and Biography*. Washington, DC: Brassey's, 1994, p. 57.

59. Matthews and Stewart, *Warriors of Christendom*, p. 60.

60. David Bongard, "History, Medieval Military," in Margiotta, ed., *Brassey's Encyclopedia of Military History and Biography*, p. 476.

Chapter 5: The Many Paths to Jerusalem

61. Jonathan Riley-Smith in "Foreword" to Malcolm Billings, *The Crusades: Five Centuries of Holy Wars*. New York: Sterling, 1996, pp. 11–12.

62. Quoted in Peters, *The First Crusade*, pp. 37–38.

63. Simon Lloyd, "The Crusading Movement," in Riley-Smith, ed., *The Oxford Illustrated History of the Crusades*, pp. 34–35.

64. John F. Sloan, "Crusades [1097–1291]." in Margiotta, ed., *Brassey's Encyclopedia of Military History and Biography*, p. 238.

65. Dupuy and Dupuy, *The Encyclopedia of Military History*, p. 312.

66. Jonathan Riley-Smith, *The Crusades: A Short History*. New Haven, CT: Yale University Press, 1987, pp. 20–21.

67. Quoted in Elizabeth Hallam, ed., *Chronicles of the Crusades*. Godalming, UK: Bramley Books, 1996, p.66.

68. Quoted in Hallam, *Chronicles of the Crusades*, pp. 173–74.

69. Quoted in Tate, *The Crusaders*, p. 117.

Chapter 6: Sword and Scimitar: Battling for God and Allah

70. Quoted in Henry Treece, *The Crusades*. New York: Barnes & Noble, 1994, p. 100.

71. Quoted in Jonathan Riley-Smith, *The First Crusade and the Idea of Crusading*. Philadelphia: University of Pennsylvania Press, 1994, p. 148.

72. Quoted in Hallam, *Chronicles of the Crusades*, p. 93.

73. Treece, *The Crusades*, p. 126.

74. Quoted in Francesco Gabrieli, ed. and trans., *Arab Historians of the Crusades*. Translated from the Italian by E. J. Costello. New York: Barnes & Noble, 1993, pp. 62–63.

75. Sloan, "Crusades [1097–1291]," in Margiotta, ed., *Brassey's Encyclopedia of Military History and Biography*, p. 239.

76. Hooper and Bennett, *The Cambridge Illustrated Atlas of Warfare*, p. 101.

77. Quoted in Gabrieli, *Arab Historians of the Crusades*, p. 216.

78. Quoted in Hallam, *Chronicles of the Crusades*, p. 193.

79. Quoted in Treece, *The Crusades*, p. 134.

80. Hallam, *Chronicles of the Crusades*, p. 199.

81. Quoted in Hallam, *Chronicles of the Crusades*, p. 223.

82. Joinville and Villehardouin, trans., with an introduction by M. R. B. Shaw, *Chronicles of the Crusades*. New York: Barnes & Noble, 1993, p. 159.

83. Treece, *The Crusades*, pp. 181–82.
84. Durant, *The Age of Faith*, p. 611.

Chapter 7: Christian Life in the Shadow of Islam

85. Tate, *The Crusaders*, pp. 63, 66.
86. Quoted in Hallam, *Chronicles of the Crusades*, pp. 77–78.
87. Quoted in Hallam, *Chronicles of the Crusades*, p. 78.
88. Treece, *The Crusades*, p. 105.
89. Quoted in Hallam, *Chronicles of the Crusades*, p. 81.
90. Durant, *The Age of Faith*, p. 591.
91. Malcolm Billings, *The Crusades: Five Centuries of Holy Wars*. New York: Sterling, 1996, p. 71.
92. Quoted in Hallam, *Chronicles of the Crusades*, p. 93.
93. Billings, *The Crusades*, pp. 71–72.
94. Jonathan Phillips, "The Latin East 1098–1291," in Riley-Smith, ed., *The Oxford Illustrated History of the Crusades*, p. 113.
95. Quoted in Billings, *The Crusades*, p. 74.
96. Treece, *The Crusades*, pp. 123–24.
97. Treece, *The Crusades*, pp. 123–24.
98. R. C. Smail, *Crusading Warfare (1097–1193)*. New York: Barnes & Noble, 1995, p. 215.
99. Dupuy and Dupuy, *The Encyclopedia of Military History*, p. 386.

Afterword: The Crusading Spirit and the March of Civilization

100. Durant, *The Age of Faith*, p. 609.
101. Quoted in Jonathan Riley-Smith, "The Crusading Movement and Historians," in Riley-Smith, ed., *The Oxford Illustrated History of the Crusades*, p. 6.
102. Lloyd, "The Crusading Movement," in Riley-Smith, ed., *The Oxford Illustrated History of the Crusades*, p. 65.
103. Durant, *The Age of Faith*, p. 612.
104. Hallam, "The New World," in *Chronicles of the Crusades*, p. 366.
105. Durant, *The Age of Faith*, p. 613.

Glossary

aumbry: A multitiered cabinet for displaying banquet service objects or food before serving.

caliph: A title given to successors of Muhammad as temporal and spiritual head of Islam.

caliphate: The office or dominion of a caliph.

carrion: Dead and decaying flesh.

Christianity: The religion derived from Jesus Christ, based on the Bible as sacred scripture and professed by Eastern, Roman Catholic, and Protestant bodies.

crusade: Any of the military expeditions undertaken by Christian powers in the eleventh, twelfth, and thirteenth centuries to win the Holy Land from the Muslims; a remedial enterprise undertaken with zeal and enthusiasm.

demesne: Land held for a lord's own use as opposed to tenured land.

destrier: Warhorse; a large, highly trained, expertly bred horse capable of carrying great loads of man and armor under horrifying battlefield conditions in medieval warfare.

Fatimids: An Arab dynasty ruling in Egypt and North Africa (909–1171), descended from Fatima and her husband Ali.

fealty: Loyalty; the fidelity of a vassal or feudal tenant to his lord.

feudalism: A method of holding land during the Middle Ages in Europe by giving one's services to the owner.

feudal lord: The master from whom men held land and to whom they owed services under the feudal system.

fief: A feudal estate; something over which one has rights or exercises control.

Franks: The Germanic tribe that conquered Gaul after the fall of the Roman Empire, whence the name France.

fuller: A cloth craftsman who cleansed and thickened newly woven fabrics.

Gaul: Ancient country in western Europe comprising chiefly the region occupied by modern France and Belgium and at one time including also the Po valley in northern Italy.

gibbet: An upright post with a projecting arm for hanging the bodies of executed criminals as a warning to others.

Holy Sepulcher: Christ's tomb in Jerusalem.

homage: An act done or payment made by a vassal in keeping his obligation to his feudal lord.

Islam: The religious faith of Muslims, including the belief in Allah as the sole deity and in Muhammad as his prophet; literally, "surrender" or "submission," hence the submission of the true believer to the will of Allah, the one God.

jihad: A holy war waged on behalf of Islam as a religious duty; a crusade for a principle or belief.

Judaism: A religion developed among the ancient Hebrews and characterized by belief in one transcendent God who has revealed himself to Abraham, Moses, and the Hebrew prophets and by a religious life in accordance with Scriptures and rabbinic traditions.

liege: A vassal bound to feudal service; a ruler or feudal lord.

Muslim: An adherent of Islam.

paradigm: Something serving as an example or model of how something should be done.

patriarch: Any of the bishops of the ancient or Eastern Orthodox sees [seats of power] of Constantinople, Alexandria, Antioch, and Jerusalem or the ancient and Western see of Rome with authority over other bishops.

Pechenegs: Nomadic Turks from the Russian steppe who once threatened Constantinople; half-brothers to the Turks in Asia Minor; also *Petchenegs*.

pier: A vertical structural support; a vertical member that supports the end of an arch or lintel, the horizontal member spanning an opening.

pogrom: An organized massacre of helpless people; specifically, such a massacre of Jews.

polytheism: Belief in or worship of more than one god.

Reconquista: The Christian reconquest of Spain in ca. 1000–1492.

Saracen: An Arab or Muslim at the time of the Crusades; a member of a nomadic people of the deserts between Syria and Arabia.

Seljuk: Of or relating to any of several Turkish dynasties ruling over a great part of western Asia during the eleventh, twelfth, and thirteenth centuries; also *Seldjuk* and *Seljuq*.

Thrace: A region in the Balkan peninsula extending to the Danube.

tracery: Architectural ornamental work, especially decorative openwork in the head of a Gothic window.

tunic: A hip-length or longer blouse or jacket.

vassal: A person under the protection of a feudal lord to whom he has vowed homage and loyalty; a feudal tenant.

wattle: A structure of interwoven sticks or twigs, often used as the underlying framework for medieval huts.

Chronology of Events

1096–1099
The First Crusade

1147–1149
The Second Crusade

1189–1192
The Third Crusade

1202–1204
The Fourth Crusade

1218–1221
The Fifth Crusade

1228–1229
The Sixth Crusade

1248–1254
The Seventh Crusade

1270–1272
The Eighth Crusade

For Further Reading

Timothy Levi Biel, *The Black Death*. San Diego: Lucent Books, 1989. Biel describes how the Black Death shattered the lives of medieval people and ultimately ended the Middle Ages.

———, *The Crusades*. San Diego: Lucent Books, 1995. The author re-creates the series of massive military campaigns that changed the Middle Ages and feudal society.

Bullfinch's Mythology, *The Age of Chivalry* and *Legends of Charlemagne*, or *Romance of the Middle Ages*. Garden City, NY: Doubleday Book & Music Clubs, n.d. This thrilling treasury brings the epic sagas and legends of the Middle Ages to life; recalls kings, knights, damsels, and noble quests.

Glyn Burgess, trans., *The Song of Roland*. London: Penguin Books, 1990. The oldest extant epic poem in French; a celebration of the crusading and feudal values of the twelfth century.

Robert Chazan, *In the Year 1096: The First Crusade and the Jews*. Philadelphia: The Jewish Publication Society, 1996. A chronicle of the events of 1096, illuminating the pogroms unleashed by the First Crusade upon the Jews in the Rhineland.

James A. Corrick, *The Early Middle Ages*. San Diego: Lucent Books, 1995. Corrick refutes the popular view that the Middle Ages were stagnant and full of superstition.

———, *The Late Middle Ages*. San Diego: Lucent Books, 1995. The author contin-

ues his treatise on the Middle Ages, covering the period from 1000 to 1500.

Eleanor Shipley Duckett, *Death and Life in the Tenth Century*. Ann Arbor: University of Michigan Press, 1991. Duckett depicts, with charm and grace, both the evils and good of the world during one of its least written about periods.

Einhard and Notker the Stammerer, *Two Lives of Charlemagne*. Translated by Lewis Thorpe. London: Penguin Books, 1969. This volume presents two fascinating, contrasting perceptions of the legendary king of the Franks and first Holy Roman emperor of western Europe.

Amy Kelly, *Eleanor of Aquitaine and the Four Kings*. New York: Book-of-the-Month Club, 1996. Kelly reveals Eleanor's greatness of vision, intelligence, and political sagacity.

Don Nardo, *Life on a Medieval Pilgrimage*. San Diego: Lucent Books, 1996. Nardo vividly re-creates the medieval world, focusing on the importance of pilgrimages.

Bradley Steffens, *The Children's Crusade*. San Diego: Lucent Books, 1991. A tragic tale of a legion of children naive enough to think that they could recapture the Holy City of Jerusalem from the Muslims in 1212 and brave enough to try.

Stephen Turnbull, *The Book of the Medieval Knight*. London: Arms and Armour Press, 1995. Turnbull tells the story of the knight during the fourteenth and fifteenth centuries—from the victories of Edward III to the fall of Richard III on Bosworth Field.

Works Consulted

Malcolm Billings, *The Crusades: Five Centuries of Holy Wars*. New York: Sterling, 1996. An authoritative look at the trials of the crusaders and the obstacles they overcame.

Charles Boutell, *Arms and Armour in Antiquity and the Middle Ages*. Translated by M. P. Lacombe. Conshohocken, PA: Combined Books, 1996. This book illustrates how armor and weaponry are closely linked to the development of tactics and the outcome of battles.

Ebenezer Cobham Brewer, *Dictionary of Phrase and Fable*, 14th ed., Ivor H. Evans, ed. New York: Harper & Row, 1989. One of the best-known and best-loved of reference books, with an astonishing range of information; a bibliophile's delight.

Norman F. Cantor, ed., *The Medieval Reader*. New York: HarperCollins, 1994. An intriguing collection of almost a hundred firsthand accounts of the medieval period.

Compton's Interactive Encyclopedia, version 3.00. Copyright © 1994, 1995, Compton's New Media. The CD-ROM version of the venerable encyclopedia.

André Corvisier and John Childs, eds., *A Dictionary of Military History*. Translated by Chris Turner. Cambridge, MA: Blackwell Publishers, 1994. A worldwide history of armed warfare, including insightful articles on crusading warfare in the Middle Ages.

Madeleine Pelner Cosman, *Medieval Wordbook*. New York: Facts On File, 1996. A volume of interesting etymological and historical facts and explanations of medieval words and phrases.

Joseph Dahmus, *A History of the Middle Ages*. New York: Barnes & Noble, 1995. Traces the continuity of the Middle Ages with ancient and modern history, illuminating events and personalities.

Hans Delbrück, *Medieval Warfare*. Vol. 3 of *History of the Art of Warfare*. Translated by Walter J. Renfroe Jr. Lincoln: University of Nebraska Press, 1990. The first modern military historian covers medieval warfare with scholarly enthusiasm.

R. Ernest Dupuy and Trevor N. Dupuy, *The Encyclopedia of Military History*. Rev. ed. New York: Harper & Row, 1977. A monumental work on warfare by two noted historians; includes an analysis of the Crusades and their effect on East-West relations.

Will Durant, *The Age of Faith: A History of Medieval Civilization—Christian, Islamic, and Judaic—from Constantine to Dante: A.D. 325–1300*. Vol. 4 of *The Story of Civilization*. New York: Simon and Schuster, 1950. A masterful survey of the achievements and modern significance of Christian, Islamic, and Judaic life and culture during the Middle Ages.

John Fines, *Who's Who in the Middle Ages*. New York: Barnes & Noble, 1995. A dictionary of biography that chronicles the lives of the men and women who dominated the time between the collapse of the Roman Empire and the Renaissance.

Francesco Gabrieli, ed. and trans., *Arab Historians of the Crusades*. Translated from the Italian by E. J. Costello. New York: Barnes & Noble, 1993. This book provides a sweeping and stimulating view of the Crusades as seen through Arab eyes.

Frances Gies, *The Knight in History*. New York: Harper & Row, 1987. The *Los Angeles Times* lauds this history as "a carefully researched, concise, readable and entertaining account of an institution that remains a part of the Western imagination."

Joseph and Frances Gies, *Life in a Medieval Castle*. New York: Harper & Row, 1974. A well-researched documentary of medieval life as rightfully centered on the castle.

——, *Life in a Medieval City*. New York: Harper & Row, 1969. An excellent account of what is known of life among medieval city dwellers.

Elizabeth Hallam, ed., *Chronicles of the Crusades*. Godalming, UK: Bramley Books, 1996. Illuminates Muslim civilization as well as the Christian West during the Holy Wars in the Middle Ages.

James Harpur, with Elizabeth Hallam, consultant, *Revelations: The Medieval World*. New York: Henry Holt, 1995. An illustrated volume that reviews the medieval period from a human perspective.

Nicholas Hooper and Matthew Bennett, *The Cambridge Illustrated Atlas of Warfare: The Middle Ages 768–1487*. New York: Cambridge University Press, 1996. An invaluable companion and guide to the role of warfare throughout the medieval period; excellent coverage of the crusading epic.

Robert Maynard Hutchins, ed., *Chaucer*. Vol. 22 of *Great Books of the Western World*. Chicago: Encyclopaedia Britannica, 1952. Contains Chaucer's *Troilus and Cressida* and *The Canterbury Tales*, with modern English versions of both works.

Joinville and Villehardouin, trans., with an introduction by M. R. B. Shaw, *Chronicles of the Crusades*. New York: Barnes & Noble, 1993. Two famous firsthand accounts of the Holy Wars, written by two noblemen who fought in the French Crusades.

Sherrilyn Kenyon, *The Writer's Guide to Everyday Life in the Middle Ages: The British Isles from 500 to 1500*. Cincinnati: Writer's Digest Books, 1995. Provides a captivating overview of life in northwestern Europe during the Middle Ages.

Franklin D. Margiotta, ed., *Brassey's Encyclopedia of Military History and Biography*. Washington, DC: Brassey's, 1994. Informative accounts of the world's great wars and the men who lead them.

John Matthews and Bob Stewart, *Warriors of Christendom: Charlemagne, El Cid, Barbarossa, Richard Lionheart*. Poole, UK: Firebird Books, 1988. The story of four great warlords from the early medieval era and how they were influenced by the chivalrous traditions that were beginning to characterize medieval culture.

A. V. B. Norman, *The Medieval Soldier*. New York: Barnes & Noble, 1993. Examines the medieval warrior's life, training, weapons and equipment, and rights and obligations under feudalism.

Geoffrey Parker, ed., *The Cambridge Illustrated History of Warfare*. New York: Cambridge University Press, 1995. A visual, detailed account of war in the West from antiquity to present.

Robert Payne, *The Dream and the Tomb: A History of the Crusades*. Chelsea, MI: Scarborough House, 1991. A splendidly wrought saga of the medieval world, from peasant's hovel to prince's palace.

Edward Peters, ed., *The First Crusade: The Chronicle of Fulcher of Chartres and Other Source Materials*. Philadelphia: University of Pennsylvania Press, 1971. A collection of literary evidence dealing with holy war and pilgrimage, including firsthand accounts of experiences by men who participated in the events of 1095–1099.

James M. Powell, *Anatomy of a Crusade 1213–1221*. Philadelphia: University of Pennsylvania Press, 1986. Powell exercises great sensitivity toward the confusion of war and the plight of leaders compelled to grapple with poorly organized armies.

Michael Prestwich, *Armies and Warfare in the Middle Ages: The English Experience*. New Haven, CT: Yale University Press, 1996. Prestwich argues that on the whole medieval warfare was no more chivalric than warfare of other periods.

Jonathan Riley-Smith, *The Crusades: A Short History*. New Haven, CT: Yale University Press, 1987. A behind-the-scenes look at the fierce battles that bloodied the sands of the Holy Land.

———, *The First Crusade and the Idea of Crusading*. Philadelphia: University of Pennsylvania Press, 1994. A view of the inner workings of the First Crusade, including organization, finances, and the division of authority and responsibility.

———, ed., *The Oxford Illustrated History of the Crusades*. New York: Oxford University Press, 1995. A handbook of the Crusades, written by a team of leading Crusade scholars.

Francis Robinson, ed., *The Cambridge Illustrated History of the Islamic World*. Cambridge, UK: Cambridge University Press, 1996. This volume surveys the whole range of Islamic history and culture, from its origins in the fifth century to the present.

Nigel Saul, ed., *Age of Chivalry: Art and Society in Late Medieval England*. London: Brockhampton Press, 1995. Medieval historians explore the nature of the society that produced and patronized the artifacts of the chivalric age.

R. C. Smail, *Crusading Warfare (1097–1193)*. New York: Barnes & Noble, 1995. Rare information on the so-called blank period in the history of the Crusades, from 1129 to 1187.

Georges Tate, *The Crusaders: Warriors of God*. Translated by Lory Frankel. New York: Harry N. Abrams, 1996. A brief but revealing tale of how the Europeans ultimately defeated themselves in the bloody two-hundred-year confrontation between two worlds.

Henry Treece, *The Crusades*. New York: Barnes & Noble, 1994. Treece describes this revolutionary period with psychological depth as well as historical accuracy and provides an unforgettable portrait of the crusaders.

Richard Vaughn, trans. and ed., *The Illustrated Chronicles of Matthew Paris: Observations of Thirteenth-Century Life*. Cambridge, UK: Alan Sutton, 1993.

A unique record of thirteenth-century life with more than a hundred full-color reproductions of the original manuscript decorations.

Philip Warner, *The Medieval Castle*. New York: Barnes & Noble, 1993. A handsomely illustrated volume explaining why and how castles were built and why they dominated medieval life.

John Alden Williams, ed., *Islam*. Vol. 5 of *Great Religions of Modern Man*. New York: George Braziller, 1962. An informative overview of the youngest of the world's great religions.

Terence Wise, *The Knights of Christ*. Vol. 155 of the Men-at-Arms series. Martin Windrow, ed. London: Osprey, 1995. A concise, informative, well-illustrated (by Richard Scollins) summary of the military orders in the Holy Land.

Index

Picture Credits

Cover photo: AKG, London

Archive Photos, 12, 54

Corbis-Bettmann, 27, 50, 56, 57, 68

Doré's Illustrations of the Crusades, Gustav Doré, Dover Publications, Inc., © 1997, 51, 63, 66, 69, 71

Giraudon/Art Resource, NY, 13, 42, 61

Heck's Pictorial Archive of Military Science, Geography and History, Ed. J. G. Heck, Dover Publications, Inc., © 1994, 16, 29, 30, 31, 41, 75

Historical Costume in Pictures, Dover Publications, Inc., © 1975, 20, 28, 34, 37, 38

Erich Lessing/Art Resource, NY, 10

Library of Congress, 17, 62

North Wind Picture Archives, 8, 18, 19, 21, 22, 23, 33, 35, 36, 58, 60, 67, 74

Jeff Paris, 40, 44

A.M. Rosati/Art Resource, NY, 26

Weapons & Armor, Ed. Harold H. Hart, Dover Publications, Inc., © 1978, 45, 48

About the Author

Earle Rice Jr. attended San Jose City College and Foothill College on the San Francisco peninsula, after serving nine years with the U.S. Marine Corps.

He has authored twenty-three books for young adults, including fast-action fiction and adaptations of *Dracula, All Quiet on the Western Front*, and *The Grapes of Wrath*. Mr. Rice has written numerous books for Lucent, including *The Cuban Revolution, The Salem Witch Trials, The Final Solution, Life Among the Plains Indians*, and seven books in the popular Great Battles series. He has also written articles and short stories, and has previously worked for several years as a technical writer.

Mr. Rice is a former senior design engineer in the aerospace industry who now devotes full-time to his writing. He lives in Julian, California, with his wife, daughter, two granddaughters, four cats, and a dog.